Tord Boontje

RIZZOLI
NEW YORK

Tord Boontje

Text by Martina Margetts
Photography by Annabel Elston and Angela Moore
Art direction of photography by Tord Boontje
Designed by Graphic Thought Facility

Foreword

This is a document of my work going back ten years.
It has been an amazing journey that started by taping
blankets to chairs made from sticks and cutting up
old wine bottles. The journey has now led me to a
place of mass production and television commercials.
Along the way I have met many supportive people
who took the risk of traveling with me.

I like working in collections, experimenting with
new thoughts, and seeking change and development,
which is a main driving force behind my work.

I believe that if we see design as a way of shaping
the future of our world, it should be as exciting and
thrilling as a great film or book. At the same time,
it should communicate not only who we are, but also
how we would ideally like our world to be.

Tord Boontje
Bourg-Argental, November 2006

"*So she sat on with closed eyes, and half believed herself in Wonderland, though she knew she had but to open them again, and all would change to dull reality.*"

Alice's Adventures in Wonderland (1865)
Lewis Carroll

Introduction

Tord Boontje is an independent industrial designer. His humanistic approach to his work is grounded in European roots and a constant alertness to the events and ideas of the day. His studio in France, a former spool-making factory, echoes Tate Modern in its stark, utilitarian beauty. It is a humming place of creativity surrounded by verdant nature, from which products are designed for industrial manufacturers and consumers on six continents.

Boontje is a hands-on designer: his childhood and education at Eindhoven and the Royal College of Art have furnished him with a sophisticated vocabulary of know-how regarding tools, materials and techniques and with an enduring and discerning appreciation of the visual arts and literature, all of which inform his projects. His love of the history of art, decoration and design coalesces with his intense interest in the future. Tradition and innovation, the handmade and hi-tech, walking and fairy tales and space travel and sci-fi, wool and latex, microchips and rocking chairs carry equal weight. He practices a kind of alchemy, investing everyday products with a sense of magic. Reality and artifice are both important.

Boontje keeps a light touch. He is serious but has the largest grin in the design world, which he uses often. He is involved long term in design issues such as sustainability and equality of opportunities in global labor and marketing, but also can react spontaneously to a design commission before he is sure how he will proceed. "Just do it" is a watchword. The vast Winter Wonderland project and the making of the Midsummer light, for example, evolved organically without drawings. The Rough-and-Ready furniture and the Garland light, two watershed projects, were born of personal experience and response to the world: design with attitude.

Boontje's independent career was inspired by the postmodern precedents of Italian and British designers, such as Memphis and Alchimia, Ron Arad and Tom Dixon. Individualistic aesthetics, rethought functions and democratizing social inclinations laid the groundwork for Boontje and others to find a personal voice in the design world, initially outside of industrial mass production. But Boontje's career has soared because he has articulated most clearly for his generation and his time the potential for industrial design to be a decorative art. He has made words such as ornament, femininity, wit, domesticity and craft—long despised in the modernist canon—powerful features of contemporary design. As the director of Kvadrat, Anders Byriel, puts it: "Tord is humanizing interiors".

The advent of new technologies such as laser-cutting and digital printing, and application of new materials have enabled Boontje to exploit his vocabulary of narrative motifs. Their sensibility reflects Boontje's engagement with literary and cinematic sources from Grimms' fairy tales and Neal Stephenson's futuristic *Snowcrash* to David Lynch movies and *Apocalypse Now*. The light/dark arena of mortality and love which Boontje's products encompass echo his generation, from the fantastical confections of Alexander McQueen and John Galliano to the mordant gestures towards the life and death of the everyday of Martin Creed, Joep van Lieshout and Damien Hirst.

Boontje is for beauty with purpose, for making everyday life better through the practice of design: he is a William Morris for our times, taking a local message and practice and transforming it for global mass consumption. There is a moral root: "life is precious," Boontje says, and in making our hearts beat faster and our minds more curious in response to his products, he achieves daily what he sets out to do: "to create a very positive, forward-looking, caring, loving world."

Martina Margetts, London, November 2006

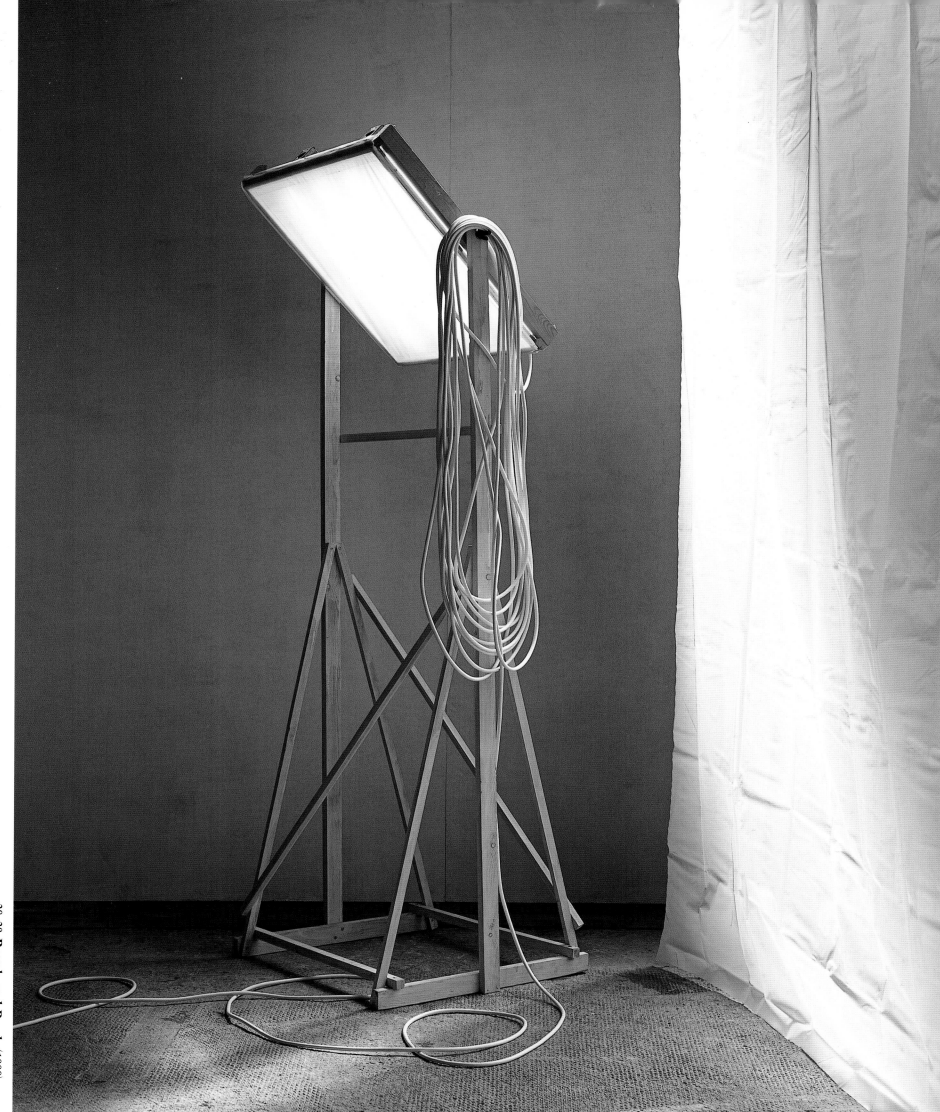

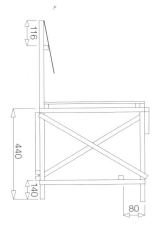

Stage 2

Stage 3

Stage 4

Building instructions for Rough-and-Ready Chair

Materials
1" x 1" softwood, or similar wood
9mm OSB plywood
32 screws N°8 x 1½"
Blanket
Strapping material

Tools
Saw
3mm drill
Screwdriver
Pencil
Tape measure

Stage 1
Cut wood for sides to length:
A Back legs, 2 off, length 847mm
B Front legs, 2 off, length 460mm
C Top horizontal side, 2 off, length 470mm
D Lower horizontal side, 2 off, length 455mm
E Side diagonal, 2 off, length 540mm

Assemble sides:
Lay front and back legs (**A** and **B**) flat.
Fix horizontals **C** and **D** in place:
      Top **C** 440mm from bottom end **A**
      Top **D** 104mm from bottom end **A**
Fix together with screws (pre-drill a hole through the softwood to prevent it from splitting)
Fix diagonal in position (**E**) as on drawing

Stage 2
Cut wood for front and back horizontals:
      For **F**, **G**, **H** and **I** 4 off, length 380mm
      For **J** 1 off, length 340mm

Fix the front and back horizontals in position with screws:
      Top **F** 116mm from top of **A**
      G and **H** on top of **C**
      I on top of **D**, 80mm from front of **D**
      J behind **A**, above **D**

Stage 3
Cut wood for front and back diagonals:
      K 1 off, 440mm
      L 1 off, 350mm
Make sure the frame is standing straight on a flat surface
Fix front and back diagonals to frame

Stage 4
Cut wood for seat and back-rest:
      Seat 450 x 380mm
      Back 250 x 380mm
      Screw seat and back to frame

Stage 5
To get the right seat angle, cut 17mm from bottom of back legs (**A**)

Stage 6
Fold blanket to size: ±1100 x 400mm
Strap blanket to frame

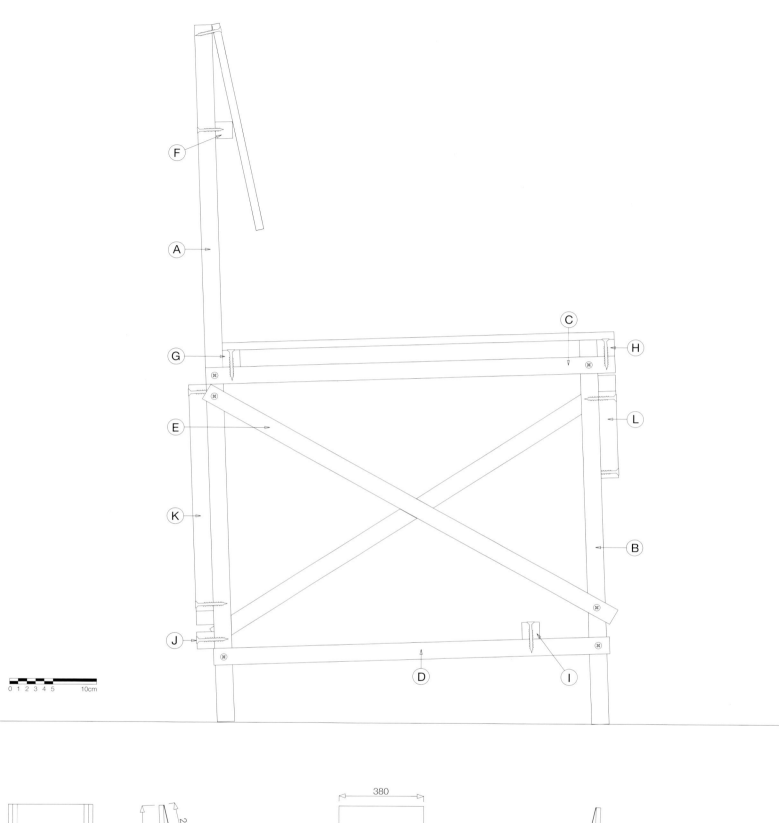

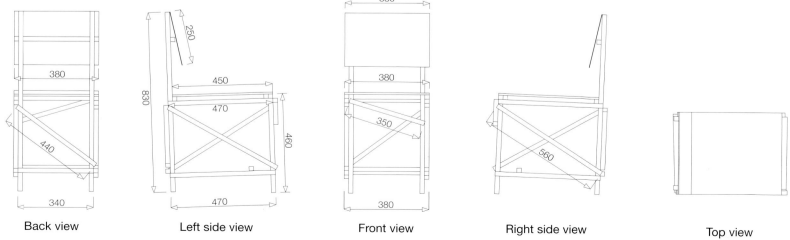

Back view   Left side view   Front view   Right side view   Top view

33. **tran$glass,** collaboration with Emma Woffenden (1997)

34–35. **tranSglass**, collaboration with Emma Woffenden (1997)

36–37. **tranSglass**, collaboration with Emma Woffenden (2006)

52–53. **Crow Chair**, Wednesday Collection (2001); **Garland Light**, Habitat (2002)

54. **Green Table** and **Bird Vase**, Wednesday Collection (2001 and 2000) 55. **Rocker**, Wednesday Collection (2003)

60, 61. **Garland Light**, Habitat (2002), Artecnica (2004)

67. **Wednesday Horse Vase** (2000) · 68 (overleaf), **Wednesday Bunny Vase** (2000) · 69 (overleaf), **Wednesday Squirrel Vase** (2000)

Being & Becoming

Books and the arts offer knowledge and ideas, tell stories and draw out emotions. Design shapes the world in tangible, non-verbal ways. Tord Boontje was born into the social and political watershed of 1968. Connecting this triangle of culture, creativity, and experience has given Boontje a singular presence in the design world in the early years of a new millennium.

How does such a designer come to be: what is the balance struck between nature and nurture? What is the culture in which the kernel of ideas can flourish and find expression? For Tord Boontje, life began in Holland in Enschede, notable only as the location for John Enschede's print works in the 1860s where he designed his remarkable typefaces and graphic borders. Home and childhood for Boontje were focused on his immediate family and the interests encouraged, above all, by his mother, Carina Edlund. "We didn't have much"[1] is the telling comment the designer makes, seeing this as the positive framing of a childhood spent making things, exploring materials in and out of doors, enjoying stories, painting, drawing, cooking. Resourcefulness, which characterizes so much of the designer's later approach, was a method of living from the earliest stage.

Boontje's parents had straightforward lives and aspirations. His Swedish mother trained and worked as a textile designer and his Dutch father was a salesman for a transport company. "He was assigned to Sweden and that's where they met and got married and moved to Holland. That's where I grew up and then for a long time my mother didn't work; she had three children," including his older sister Cindie and younger brother Adri, the three of them each eighteen months apart.

Throughout his childhood he was actively creative, his mother recalls. "If it was a rainy day all the children around us were coming to us and we were making things, drawings, cutting out houses and roads for cars." She also helped at her children's school in the early years, teaching them and others textile techniques in the creativity hours, "one year knitting, one year embroidery." The freedom experienced in these childhood years has allowed Boontje to place a premium on experimentation and hands-on drawing and making in the development of ideas.

The aspect of making filtered from his maternal grandparents—his grandfather an engineer and inventor, his grandmother a weaver. Holidays with them at their house in Bromma near Stockholm were a source of pleasure and influence, full of looms, books, workshops and open space to roam freely. While they had guinea pigs or a cat at home, out in nature his mother remembers, "we were very open and tried to look at the birds or see if a mouse or bigger animal was there." Boontje confirms: "We loved going there at summer and Christmas; we were always very excited."

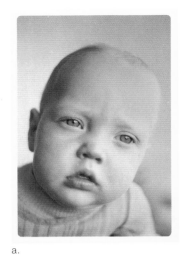

a.

b.

a. Tord at eight months.

b. The house of Carina Edlund,
Tord's mother, in Sweden.

The turning point in this early unbroken sense of well-being came with the separation of his parents when Boontje was six years old, an amicable but eventually final parting of the ways. Something of his resilience and flexibility seems to have lodged from that time. "It was a shock for us, but also as a child you're put in a position—because it's not your choice—you somehow have to choose sides. I had a great loyalty towards my mother and it was in some ways a difficult time. But then we moved to a new house in the same town, Zevenaar, which we thought was exciting: completely modern, the second house in a row of houses with big windows and a little back yard, one of the first houses in this whole new neighborhood that was finished, and the rest was like one huge building site. It was a great opportunity for us to come home every day covered in mud."

"I started school at the age of six. After my parents divorced I moved to another school. I can remember feeling very nervous about changing school and missing my friends. The new school was further away, a long cycle ride. In the morning we'd all cycle together with my mother and she'd pick us up at lunchtime, cycle home, and then she'd take us back to school together, through wind and snow." The period was an important watershed in sensing a degree of unconventionality, which has allowed Boontje to feel he can challenge the status quo and do things differently: "between my years of six and eight, my mother had Dutch lessons intensively in speaking and writing. We very much picked up on the fact that we were not like other children. You feel different. I was always quite comfortable. I thought, 'I'm different; I'm part Swedish and I'm being brought up without a father.'"

The pragmatic optimism inherent in Boontje's present approach to life was established from early days. "It was very much: if we need a table, well, we'll make a table. Where we stored our bicycles we had a little workbench where my brother and I made things. We loved being there; we were always, always making things. We didn't have a car. For a long time we didn't have a telephone. But we were very happy as well; we were a very strong kind of family," a unit his best friend Ben Panayi describes as "very tribal."

When he was around ten or eleven he asked his mother to knit a jumper he had designed on a small piece of paper. He was precise about the color, the size—and the motif: "a lot of flowers, fantasy flowers," she says. The love of flowers, his mother feels, is his natural self, "they're a part of his life." When he came to his mother to knit the jumper she said, "I was surprised, but I thought if he asked that I will try to do that for him; as a mother you must try to do that."

The close influence of his mother, always destined to be strong through circumstances, has been decisive not only for emotional and creative, but also for cultural and social reasons. Needing to find a means of supporting her family, she found that for some reason the Dutch authorities did not accept her Swedish diplomas, so she re-trained as a teacher in the histories of costume, textiles, and art. The books and materials with which she surrounded herself at home became the tools for Boontje's early education in art and in research: "in that period she was studying, there was always a huge amount of books around, and she was always writing essays and doing research. If we had to do a project for school, she would always help us, she would teach us how to use books, how to go to the library, how to find information." This whole sense of researching was there from a very early age, but also opening up a world of ideas through art, science, nature and fairy tales, which she read to all three children from early on. The table spread with books, papers and pictures, the garden outside, a space to make things, his mother someone to initiate conversations and long explorations of nature on 300-kilometer bicycle rides and camping holidays to cherished country sites ("We loved it there, absolutely loved it")—these were the healthy infusions of insight into the human imagination and natural wonders.

The attentiveness to detail, closely observing animals and botany, springs from those years, and he notices it in his young daughter Evie now. The moral framework, of giving and taking pleasure in equal measure through personal effort, of caring for people and the environment, of living with things made by hand, has remained vital to Boontje's purpose. This sense of family is the pulse of his life, metaphorically reflected in the families of works he has produced in series as a methodology in his career.

The values his mother describes resonate with Boontje. Since 1999, she has lived ninety minutes from Stockholm in Sala, bounded by forest on three sides and open views to the north, a place Boontje visits annually with his wife, glass artist Emma Woffenden, and Evie. His mother, inspired by place, believes that what is important is "peace in the world, that I specially find in nature—in the nature I see the forms and the colors and the energy. I go every day for one hour into the forest; it will be peace. If I find a wounded bird I take it with me and try to give it a new life. I weave and re-use the materials of old clothes. You don't need to buy a lot of expensive things, but you can give old things a new life." Boontje's own views on the environment today are emphatic: "what's happening will get worse unless we change it. We're all responsible and all need to do something." He thinks carefully about food, about labor conditions in his own studio and beyond, and about ethical behavior, but always with humor and a positive outlook. "Life is precious," he says.

While his mother prescribes peace at the micro level—"around me I have a lot of old people and families with young children; I try to take care of them"—Boontje, growing up in Holland, remembers the wish for peace in a wider political arena. The Holland he grew up in still bore the effects of the uncomfortable demarcation between the Protestant north and Catholic south, "completely separate, newspapers, TV stations, everything divided," which was only finally eroded by the government actively moving ministries and utility companies. There were also housing problems in the cities, "a big squatters' movement," and in his mid-teens at school, "I was very outspoken in my political and social views," visiting the older siblings of school friends in the cities at weekends and seeing big demonstrations. "From a young age I was very politically aware, from aged twelve I read the newspaper every day. I grew up too late to be affected by the Vietnam era; it didn't shape my thinking about the world, but we were anti nuclear weapons and anti Reagan," (then President of the United States). There were big discussions about cruise missiles, "a lot of protest and debate" and the demonstration he attended in Amsterdam involved a million people and helped stop the missiles coming to Holland.

As he grew, Boontje was broadening the possibilities for self-expression, entertaining himself and others. Besides dens, bookshelves, lights, he made and wore an earring a day and his mother remembers "a stream of girls were coming to buy the earrings from him." His room changed color. His hair changed color. For a year he dressed only in red, white or black. He went to discos from the age of thirteen—"black lights, white glossy floors, ultraviolet light, no trainers allowed and really boring music"—and later to clubs, where he worked occasionally behind the bar or as a DJ. Here was a group of like-minded friends who screenprinted posters for concerts, wore a lot of black, and enjoyed music they could dance to or whose lyrics "had real meaning and said something about your life": The Cure, Simple Minds, U2, the Smiths. All the experimentation was characteristically playful rather than beyond the edge.

The picture darkened in 1983, when at the age of fifteen his mother became ill. This, together with the divorce of his parents, is a central shaping experience of his early life, just as, later, is the union with Emma and the birth of his daughter.

"My mother became ill. The doctors didn't know what it was. A kind of trapped nerve in her spine." Boontje suggests it arose from the demands of her life. "She had three jobs, three children, no car, carrying heavy bags all the time, bicycling a long way. She was in a wheelchair for a year. We had to do everything in the house, my brother, sister, and I. We went through a lot together as children, we had to contribute to running the household and look after each other. We definitely had to work together as equals." Eventually, his sister left to study art in Arnhem, while his brother did operational factory jobs and also worked as a stand-up comedian, clown, and magician, echoing the laughter he brought about in childhood for his siblings. From seeing each other perhaps twice a year for a long period, more recently their lives have crossed paths, to the extent that his brother helped him this year on the building of **Winter Wonderland** p.232–233 for Swarovski and may collaborate further from his new design construction workshop in Poland. His sister, having also trained as a medical assistant, is now moving back to painting alongside life with children in Holland. "Now we'll all have our own country," Boontje laughs.

The solicitous affection for his siblings and mutual respect regarding creativity and personal space is palpable. Boontje learnt a kind of self-reliance, sustained self-containment, a willingness to help others, a generosity of spirit. Eventually his mother recovered but by then his childhood years were over and he had determined to leave home and study design.

This was not a foregone conclusion from his interests at school, where his main subjects were English, Dutch, Math, Biology, Chemistry, and Physics. Studying Physics was even a possibility, though "more like a plan B. Strangely enough, I didn't choose Art as a subject. I loved art at home but in school it was quite formal, led by rules and grades and that way of dealing with art didn't appeal to me." Since he read so much his mother thought he might study history, but he also said at one point "I will be a weatherman." Then he wanted to go to new places where people hadn't been before, an abiding interest in space which Boontje still discusses and his friend Panayi alluded to when I asked what Boontje would be doing in the future—"living on the moon."

The decision to study design grew from his grandfather's influence, his pleasure in making things himself and the design collection in the museum at Arnhem, which made him aware it could be a profession. His mother's view is that "by the age of 13 or 14 he knew it was a good way, to be a designer, and I thought it was" and by the time of applying "he was 100%."

He thought about studying in Arnhem or Amsterdam, but decided on Eindhoven after a talk at his school by an old boy who was a graduate. The application and interview were then straightforward: "I was feeling very confident. I knew exactly what I was doing. I was just really *enthusiastic*." This is unsurprising since throughout his childhood "I had designed my whole environment." This was a turning point in Boontje's life and he embraced all the opportunities it afforded him.

Eindhoven has been a continuously dynamic think-tank for design students, producing graduates alongside Boontje whose work shows the hallmark of lateral design thinking and material versatility, such as his near contemporaries Hella Jongerius and Jurgen Bey. But the aim of the course, led for thirty years by the worldly and distinguished textile designer Ulf Moritz, who had worked in the Beatles Apple building in London and knew the artist Christo, was to produce designers not artists; painting was taught as a drafting method not for its own sake. Artists Boontje learned of, such as Anselm Kiefer and Willem de Kooning , impressed him for their insights into texture and color. The level of practical engagement with skills and materials was high. All the tutors also worked in industry. Boontje seized on opportunities to experiment with scale, function and thinking around the body within a theme of Man and Identity, which Moritz recommended to him as being "more haptic, more poetic" than the other themes around mobility, living and the public realm.

In a mellifluous German accent, Moritz remembers Boontje "at the start as a very gentle, kind boy, very thin, very young, with blue eyes, a good presence in his eyes. As a student he was innovative. He was the most intelligent and intellectual designer there and very sympathetic, but he didn't show it—very Dutch." A scent bottle project impressed Moritz so much "I told him, 'You must go to Paris.'"

His tutor Joke Visser van der Heyden, "my favourite teacher," has left an enduring impression, for the projects she set and for her critical rigour: "You got on with her or not." As Boontje describes her, "she was this real mysterious character: she lived in a Rietveld house in the forest and would drive to Eindhoven in this fiberglass car; she'd get out wearing clogs and had holes in her clothes, carrying a handbag with weird things inside." She had a striking reputation: the story goes that her future husband resolved to meet her when he heard she had lined her walls at home with eggshells.

A project might involve choosing a person out of *Interview* magazine and designing a house for them. "Her way of teaching was always to say 'do a bit more, experiment more, do more tests. Why don't you go home and come back next week?' You were learning so much that she would say something and at first you wouldn't understand and then a few weeks later you did." Both Moritz and Visser van der Heyden rejected projects if they didn't feel the students' ideas were new enough. "It was all about developing your own thinking and realizing that work is a vehicle to translate thoughts about the way the world is and what it should be," says Boontje. Visser van de Heyden herself acknowledges that she set high standards, but believes the interaction with students is always "a kind of a game," knowing how a push can elicit the right reaction. "I wanted to let them discover things, to experiment as much as possible. No rules."

Visser van der Heyden remembers a "very fresh and very open young man, young and grown up together" who "really wanted to do the job," and "a man full of poetry, very interested in what was going on around him." When she saw his assiduously researched pearlescent paint project, which used magnets to create patterns, developed on placement at Akzo-Nobel, she "realized he could go far." He had "marvelous ideas about how you could do things differently." But she says she "had no idea of what he might become" and that "he himself was open, he worked with the situation he was in." But she knew he had the Dutch designers' characteristic she observed and encouraged in over thirty years of teaching: "They experiment a lot," like the "astonishing Droog Design and Moooi."

At Eindhoven, Boontje had experience of ceramics and textiles, two disciplines fundamental to his current production, and a host of other materials including wood, metal, plastic, paper. He successfully learned the ceramics techniques including turning and slipcasting, but had variable experience with textiles, even after a later year studying them at Winchester School of Art in England in 1989. ("There I liked the emphasis on a direct personal approach to design and the link with function, and the teachers, but I had the strong feeling that I didn't want to be a textile designer"). Paradoxically, the success of his Wednesday collection and virtuoso collaborations with Kvadrat, for example, shows how much the textile language speaks to him.

The opportunities of internships during his Eindhoven years were also

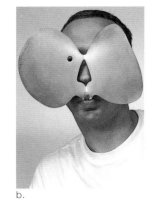

a.   b.   c.

critical to the development of Boonje's approach to both the nature and the business of design. He knew he must find out what kind of career he wanted to have and set off for New York with a portfolio and a contact. Certainly his portfolio got him noticed—a huge polycarbonate and aluminum, rubber-spined object in a city where "everyone walks around with a black portfolio. In the elevator, people would ask where I was going and said, 'well, if it doesn't work out there, come to us!'" The skill of eye-catching presentation was already evident.

Boontje knocked on doors for two weeks, showed his work and was taken on for three months at a commercial architects' office. By the end, he knew this was not how he wanted to work. The projects were big but tightly briefed and controlled, the staff extensive, the freedom restricted, the approach conventional. The New York experience was "very important. I very strongly realized then: that's not what I want to do after I graduate." He left New York and was happy to return there on very different terms for his first solo show in the States at Moss Gallery in 2005.

The New York job did not appeal, but the city did. Boontje's love of what the writer Jay McInerney termed *Bright Lights, Big City*, where high art and popular culture mix with glamour, street cred, and architectural beauty, stays with him as an enthusiasm even while nature, siren-like, always calls him back.

The second internship was entirely different. Through a contact again, he got the chance to work at the epicentre of postmodernism, Alessandro Mendini's Studio Alchimia in Milan. "It was the opposite of my New York experience. If there is no project, well, make a project. It was a whole different motivation, not about making money. I felt I fitted in to that group. I was really appreciated." The combination of qualities in the studio which the iconic designer, architect, and theorist had established in 1976, matched Boontje's inclinations: "an artist's form of design, done with a writer's wit and making cultural references with a sophistication that has rarely been achieved in furniture." [2]

There were some satirical moments. Boontje recalls with amusement running across Milan clutching the model made from designs by Ettore Sottsass for an exhibition of "house gods." On arriving at the office of the great designer—"a really, really nice friendly man, really calm, incredibly slow. Exactly how you would imagine"—the first thing the youthful Boontje saw was Sottsass taking a knife to the penis Sottsass had playfully supplied in the original sample. More ambitiously, Boontje worked on the Groningen Museum, the landmark building of Mendini's approach to design.

Perhaps surprisingly, Boontje remembers the atmosphere there was "really, really quiet," with an upstairs gallery with big windows painted bright green. He worked on exhibitions and made Seurat-like paintings on paper for transfer to furniture surfaces: "The whole studio environment was completely like a Memphis space."

In practice, Mendini was less present for Boontje. Alessandro Guerriero was his mentor there, giving him a letter when he left saying he would become *"un grande progettista,"* which Boontje viewed as "a great encouragement." The

d.

a. Presentation for color research project, Eindhoven.

b, c. Mask for Looking Backwards, first project at RCA.

d. RCA class on summer visit to B&B Italia.

e. Emma and Tord in Venice, 1995.

e.

potential he experienced in Milan, to exercise freedom in design direction, to be individualistic, to challenge the status quo, affected him deeply and sowed the seeds of the design approach he wanted to pursue. There were three crucial aspects of design which were coalescing: the invention of a personal language, epitomized by Sottsass and Andrea Branzi of Memphis; social awareness and values, exemplified by Superstudio's work such as the 1970s film of people living underground; and the ability to sustain a business, characterized by Philippe Starck, the enduring French design superstar, whom Boontje admires not always for his design ideas but for "the scale of the output and to be at the top and stay at the top for fifteen years."

The stimulation of the Eindhoven course persuaded him that further study was necessary to open out the cultural and theoretical framework in which he could mature. The Royal College of Art (RCA) in London was, he felt, the only place, since at the time no equivalent postgraduate design course existed in Holland. Boontje describes this period of study as one of great happiness and excitement. "I knew what to expect there. I had been to open days, to degree shows. I had a really good time there. I knew my way around college very quickly—fashion, ceramics and glass, photography."

"The other students were as motivated as me and they made really interesting things and you could push each other to improve. Every day you could go and hear fantastic lectures that made you think about your approach to your work and you learned interesting references, whether it was about film or jewellery or theory. I was like a big sponge—the whole culture of it, the philosophy, practice, how they inform each other and connect." Influentially, his Professor of Industrial Design was the remarkable Daniel Weil, now a design

a–l. Early concept models for eyewear project, RCA. Photographed with fellow students and tutors modeling:
a. Robert
b. Thomas Dahinten
c. Dai Rees
d. Caroline
e. Stuart Aldridge
f. Netta Marciano
g. Chris Parker
h. Moche Marciano
i. Jane Dillon
j. Ben Panayi
k. Jackie Piper
l. Chris Lefteri

m–p. RCA degree projects:
m. Oval bed with adjustable ring.
n. Eyewear that shades the eyes and maintains eye contact.
o. Double-skinned wine cooler.
p. Double-skinned porcelain tableware.

q. Graduation with Daniel Weil.

partner at Pentagram, who "for the first time made me see that design could be a cultural activity" and who blurred the boundaries between art, craft, and design, couched in theoretical discourse. Boontje also met Emma there who, he avers, "has been very influential for everything I have done."

Weil was pleased to select Boontje: "He had a good lineage, a very anarchic lineage. I enjoyed his energy, his anarchy...he had something that would benefit from having an opportunity to develop his own point of view. I thought he would be perfect. He was perfect."

The investigations into materials, structures, surfaces, and technologies were systematically thought through in these two postgraduate years. "The RCA," he says, "gave a very strong global perspective on what we do...The Alessi project was important because we visited the factory and I could see it was not so different to an artisan workshop, it was approachable and really interested in ideas and new things." Boontje made a sinuous, articulated metal fruit bowl, winning the approval of Alberto Alessi himself, and which already revealed the inspiration of fairy tales on his designs, in this case *The Little Prince*, with the drawing of the snake and the lump inside of the eaten boy. The Alessi project

m.

n.

o.

p.

q.

still resonates with Boontje now, because it was building up a narrative language of products and "really made me understand the subtleties of tableware."

Boontje produced three projects for his degree show, eyeshades, double-skinned ceramic tableware and a rotating bed, all related to the body on different scales, with the qualities of "friendliness, softness, informality." Weil appreciated that his student sought to "investigate the fundamentals of life" by finding "popular solutions." The fact that he made a full-sized bed as opposed to a scale model or drawing, Weil says, "demonstrated the energy that he had within him; demonstrated that he had no fear. He had that very interesting edge, that layer of popularizing, banalizing the fundamentals, to be that intellectual non-intellectual, the Damien Hirst patina, in a way." (Interestingly, the emphasis on construction and new materials and technology in the work at the time "later," Boonjte explains, "became much less important and my work started to come much more out of a kind of energy which was sometimes formally less elegant and sometimes more sinister. But it wasn't a stylistic decision to work like that!")

Although seen as a star by tutors and peers (his friend Ab Rogers calls him "a prolifically successful student"), on graduating in 1994 he did not immediately know what he was going to do. Boontje laughs at the contrast in the early nineties with Eindhoven where "you are at college, you leave college, you work. Leaving the RCA is a big shock. No, you don't get the job or the commission!" even though during your time at the RCA "you really live there 24/7; a working environment."

Although Boontje and Emma, a firm partnership from college onwards, were by their own admission extremely "work-orientated," they took pleasure in what metropolitan life offered—lots of parties with friends, drinking and bacchanalian dancing, going to clubs (the Milk Bar, Wag Club), "visiting four exhibitions on a Sunday in the car," picnics on Hampstead Heath, and going

a.

b.

every two years to the Venice Biennale. Years later on their wedding day, Boontje and Emma arrived at their reception at the Barrett Marsden Gallery with all their friends on a double-decker Routemaster bus to the boisterous music of the Latin American band awaiting them.

In the year between Eindhoven and the RCA, Boontje had worked for Moritz on exhibition installations and continued his own paint color research. "From day one I was busy and earning money." So after the RCA he again worked for Moritz on shop and exhibition designs in Holland and then teamed up with fellow RCA graduate Moshe Marciano to do similar projects in London. The partnership did not last. Boontje had tried again with his magnetic paints project; he had tried numerous companies with his other ideas, including Wedgwood, Rosenthal and Iittala, but without success, "nice but not for us." But he was never deflected from wanting to make his way. Panayi remembers dejectedly saying, "Tord, I see myself living in a cardboard box underneath a bridge. Do you ever worry? And he's saying 'I'm not going to let that happen.'" Boontje says: "There's this part of struggling to generate work for companies...OK, I stop doing all this, I'm not going to wait for anybody and I will take control. It was very slow and frustrating, but at the same time a really important realization got formed."

The significance of the designer Ron Arad as "hero" is important. Boontje had been startled by his concrete sound system exhibited in Rotterdam in 1989, but also it is Arad and his generation in the early 80s who showed that the individualistic "ad hoc" approach to a career was not only desirable but possible. As Arad says, "I invented my own profession." Boontje was also impressed by the strongly independent approach to life of fashion designer Alexander McQueen, for whom he designed eyewear and watches for several years from 1998: "I knew he was doing well and self-made, and I could really relate to that. I thought: this is what I want to do." This achievement was just on the horizon.

Boontje was becoming part of a loose mix of designers, some with a craft training, who determined to go into production with their ideas on their own initiative, some of whom were selected to exhibit together: Michael Marriott, Jane Atfield, Precious McBane, BarberOsgerby, Inflate, el ultimo grito. He began to work more closely with Emma in her glass studio. By this time, her own career was developing strongly in the area of fine art practice, but the equipment for glass cutting, grinding, and polishing in the studio inspired them to think of using existing glass material and reworking it in some way. Glass wine bottles, available everywhere in recycled bottle units, provided the answer and in 1997 their glass product collection **tranSglass**[p. 34–37] was born, achieving a kind of alchemy with the transformation of discarded objects into useful things of contemporary beauty.

The crucial development for Boontje was to have produced work that attracted both commercial and cultural recognition. This started him thinking more about recycling and its language and the **Rough-and-Ready**[p. 25—31] collection evolved as a "reaction to Milan—so slick. I felt so much an outsider. I felt this

c.

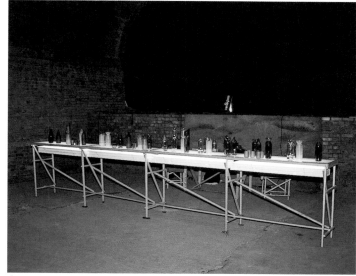

a. Studio Unit 19, Rushworth Street.

b. Home in Peckham Rye with Rough-and-Ready high chair.

c. Installation at Tate Modern, London, 2001.

d. Stand at Designers Block, London 1999.

d.

is not for me; this is for another world. This is not how I want to live." The impact of tranSglass and Rough-and-Ready in the latter nineties brought Boontje the press attention and the affirmation of cultural significance that represented a key stage of development in his career. (Boontje recounts the surreal experience of "one day knocking up some bits of furniture and a couple of months later they're collected in a truck for Tate Modern along with Francis Bacons" for *Century City: Art and Culture in the Modern Metropolis* in February 2001.)

Wider recognition followed the launch of Wednesday. It was after Evie's birth that Boontje, his wife, and daughter spent six weeks at his mother's house near Stockholm. "I think," says his mother, "he was searching his way and after Evie was born he found it. There was a new chapter in his life and he became calmer and he was thinking a lot." With the Wednesday collection of 2001, she feels he established a design language "between fantasy and reality, a world most people don't get into" but who are glad someone does this on their behalf. In nature "the contrasts between snow and meadows, leafless branches and icicles" is something Boontje himself alludes to, and these evoke the metaphorical

a.

b.

a. Wedding Day.

b. The Bakehouse studio in Peckham, London.

c. Preparing *Happy Ever After* in the Bakehouse.

d. Constructing the Princess Chair with an 1850s Victorian frame and 60 meters of silk organza.

e. Traveling to Monaco with Evelyn, Emma, Laure Grezard and Rugiada Petrelli.

fh. Interview during *Happy Ever After* exhibition.

imagery of a light and dark side evident in his work. His mother continues, "flowers are very different in summertime to winter, you can see the positive and the negative in everything" and says of the light/dark polarity, "that's life. You are not so happy all the year every day. It's a sort of balance." Andree Cooke, who had commissioned the exhibition from Boontje that resulted in Wednesday, shown in the Window Gallery in Prague, said simply: "I thought, this will make his career." She was right.

Despite critical acclaim, income was low and Boontje started teaching. He abandoned the proposed move to teach at Falmouth by the sea in the west of England in favor of an invitation from Ron Arad, Professor of Design Products at the RCA, whom he had finally met a couple of years before: "I had just had a little baby. I had no clients, no work, nothing at that time, so then Ron came up to me when we did Designers' Block. He said he'd seen the exhibition *Stealing Beauty* and he really liked it, which I was amazed by because it was the first time I'd spoken with Ron. A really nice moment for me."

Boontje initially taught in the Design Products department with Michael Marriott and Jasper Morrison. His friend Marriott enumerates the qualities that made Boontje popular: "lots of enthusiasm, lots of perception, lots of knowledge, lots of different ways of stuff being done and an interest in sharing it all." Boontje then taught with Ab Rogers, who had graduated from the RCA in 1997 and taught for four years at Leeds. "We shared passions and excitements" says Rogers, a close friend who had first got to know him through his wife Sophie, a chef and friend of Emma's, even though there were "great similarities and great differences," his own work using a high finish and slick materials with physical movement and interaction but recognising that Boontje, with tranSglass, was cleverly "converting poor materials into slick product." Rogers "designs through art direction, I need people to make, whereas Tord is very hands on."

Julie Mathias, a student of theirs and now a rising designer in her own right, describes the experience: "The platform" (the department's term for a tutor group) "was about an evolution. The view was that it's not about the platform, it's more about working as an individual. Some on the platform were more technological, but Tord respects any kind of design because as a student himself he was much more industrial."

Rogers outlines the broad theme as "decoration and technology" and design objects as sensations. "We were consciously trying to encourage students into action. Tord's work is much more about a quest than finding a single style." A great project was creating "sensory tools" with one student making a kit for stealing human hair, and candles containing hair that sprouted as the candle burned down. They took students to Tate Modern to the Rebecca Horn show with the upside down suspended piano and watched the McQueen video of spray-painting on a white dress to think about machines to create decoration;

c.

d.

e.

f.

students made a three-course meal exploring smell, tactility, and Boontje recalls, "bonbons crushed in your mouth making different sounds," culminating in a party with vodka in frozen half lemons, "a fantastic thing, a disposable glass."

Mtthias tellingly describes another project: "at the start of the year, there was a very quick one-week project: we had to do something in our home. Most brought their projects in but I invited everyone to my flat because my home is on the 21st floor of a windy council block, a huge tower with big windows. I had connected all the lights in my flat with the wind outside, so that during dinner the lights went up and down according to the level of wind. I wanted it to be really scary, but it wasn't, it was beautiful." The beauty in the work is Tord's influence: "I always wanted to make it scary and he made it beautiful, the balance is thanks to him. He impressed me with the idea that design has to be something that you would like to look at."

As a teacher "you could show him any beginning and he would get enthusiastic and think about it and answer later. He was always giving a lot of information, really looking into your projects. There were never things he disliked, he aimed to be in your direction. He also helped students working: I was working on lampshades using fiberglass bandages; he tried it. He's always doing and trying and not scared about getting something done."

Boontje's own commentary reflects his aims. "One thing I was very clear about was that I had to really get to know the students and really, really listen to them. Some tutors don't really know you or your projects and were more interested in telling you what great things they'd done." Ron Arad, as Course Director, appreciated Boontje's range: "I think he was a great tutor because he's done sunglasses, industrial design, he's an active creator, and there's something good about people who encourage others."

From 2001 to 2004 in London , Boontje's studio became increasingly busy and he eventually gave up teaching. He recalls the dynamics of that period: "In these years the team varied in size between four and eight people, depending on the projects that were going on. Most people working in the Bakehouse studio were students and former students from the RCA, Design Products, Textiles, and Fashion." The main people were Joe Nunn, his first assistant, Jodi Mullen, studio manager, and designers Asuka Koda, Laure Grezard and Carmel McElroy and there were projects for Swarovski, Moroso, Dartington Crystal, Authentics, and Artecnica. "The studio was crowded with everyone working in a space that

Picnic in the forest with Emma,
Evelyn and Tord's mother, Carina.

was filled with drawings, samples, materials and computers. Although full, it was also a very inspiring environment to work in. I like this fluidity between the computers and the hands-on material experience. Things can cross over very seamlessly when you place a computer, a pot of resin, some embroidery yarns, and a vice next to each other."

Boontje was fascinated by the impact of a growing reputation. "This was also a time during which we noticed a big change in perception. Suddenly journalists from all over the world would find their way to Peckham to see what was going on there. There was something very striking about the contrast of the rough south-London Peckham environment and people from Hermes, Swarovski, the *New York Times,* and *Vogue* visiting us. I realized very strongly that something had changed when one morning I was whisked off to Austria in a private plane to discuss a new project with Swarovski. Or after staying in Abu Dhabi in five-star hotels with private drivers, following an invitation to make lighting concepts for a new mosque, and returning to London to go back to work the next day on the 312 bus."

Prizes recognized his reputation. Boontje was shortlisted for the Design Museum's first Designer of the Year prize in 2003, he was *Elle Decoration* Designer of the Year in 2003 and won best product design at the New York Gift Fair in 2004, to add to the Bombay Sapphire prize for the Blossom chandelier for Swarovksi and glassware with Dartington of 2002. But the quality of life he hoped for did not seem to present itself in London. Emma had always wanted to leave the country, planning to go after graduating from the RCA, and by 2004 it had become urgent to think about it again if they were to find more space, peace and a natural environment.

"I felt I would really ideally like to live in the forest" is the way Boontje begins the story of how he, Emma and Evie finally came to find themselves leaving London for southern France in March 2005. His international client base and the technology of emails and mobiles also freed him from a London base. Laure Grezard, a French assistant in the Bakehouse, suggested the region of her childhood; in a selection process worthy of the Goldilocks fairy tale, they had considered Sweden, "too cold," the south of France, "too hot" and Holland "too boring" before finding the verdant region around St Etienne, about an hour from Lyons, with rolling valleys, quiet villages, livestock, and hills covered in

Still from TV commercial, Target,
Christmas 2006.

pine forests. They had driven around for five days and, says Emma, "We kept coming back because we like those trees," one Douglas fir in particular acting like a beacon to draw them there.

"I believe some people are seaside coast types and some people are forest types" Boontje says. They had noted the phone number of an old factory they had seen in the village of Bourg-Argental and when Grezard phoned, the owner told them they would have to come that weekend because he was ready to sell to others on Monday. In a fateful moment, Boontje decided "Let's just go. So we hopped on a plane." They still had no idea of the building's interior, thinking it was "lots of small rooms and two floors, and probably would need a lot of work." When the door opened and they looked inside and saw the open space "it was just, like, *wow*." Emma adds: "We fell in love with the roof and the windows because they started at three meters off the floor and there was my lighted cell I'd been looking for." Peals of laughter follow Boontje's blindingly optimistic summary that, "it was perfectly dry inside and we thought, well, it doesn't need anything doing to it. Let's buy it."

Despite trying to learn French in London, both had very limited ability. Boontje recalls, "We got the whole French contract translated by Google, which kept trying to translate my name and talked about the left-handed house." When the notaries insisted on the ten per cent deposit as they finalized the sale before Christmas 2004, they experienced the notorious obduracy of French banks and had to run between cash points to try and start raising the money. Eventually, they were given the smallest key they had ever seen from the huge hands of the farmer owner, "went to the Hotel de France and had a nice glass of wine."

Having as usual acquired a studio before a house, they rented a flat, installed Grezard and another assistant to help, and set about getting water, electricity, and toilet put into the cavernous studio. It was freezing cold, and with no heating Boontje wrestled with French bureaucracy from a makeshift cupboard space, his resilience and determination sustaining him once more. "I felt like a janitor in the cupboard, but at least he gets out to sweep the corridors and I'm bound here by this phone, dealing with post and French papers and English tax. I stayed in the cupboard a good three months, after which I came out and wouldn't touch a piece of paper any more."

At the same time, Boontje was preparing new work for Moroso, the Shiseido *Karakusa* exhibition, his first in Japan, and the launch of the fabric collection for Kvadrat. And just before they moved to France, Target, one of the largest retail companies in the USA, had called, so the massive project, involving a total "new look" and product range for Christmas 2006 was also under way. Elated, Boontje went out and bought a new black Saab cabriolet for himself and a Volkswagen Golf for Emma. The future at last seemed assured.

But the long trajectory of becoming a man, a designer, a professional, a husband, and a father could be metaphorically summarized by the move to France. "We'll make it happen" and "Just do it" are watchwords for Boontje, who has the single-minded perseverance, the imagination, the courage and familial inspiration to forge his own path. In London, at home in their rented Peckham flat, they had had a map of France on the wall for a long time, they had taken lessons at the Institut Français in South Kensington, they had been encouraged by Evie's brave encounters with children she didn't know at campsites to believe she would manage a new school in a strange country, they had found their forest, and they were supported by family and friends, even though some, like Ben and Ab, were excited but "scared for them."

When, on 29th March 2005, the day came to leave London, the city that had nurtured all his ambitions, Boontje remembers the removers "came with three people, but by lunchtime they had called up another eight people. It was a massive operation" and Emma's kiln kept collapsing on its wheels. "We moved everything over to France in the biggest truck you could possibly get with the biggest trailer, bigger than the truck itself, so big they couldn't pull the whole thing up over the mountains. So they had to park the trailer, unload the truck and then get the trailer, just to manage all Emma's big machines." They had been phoned by a magazine to cover the move, but wisely Boontje had decided "some things you should keep private." They traveled by Eurostar themselves, arrived, unloaded everything in the flat, the garage and finally in the studio.

Boontje ends the story with a sense of his own destiny fulfilled: "I remember really strongly: they drove off and there we were with our things in this big building with the doors open, seeing this truck disappear round the corner. And I thought, OK, that's it, we're here."

1. All quoted speech throughout this section is from individual interviews with Martina Margetts, author of the text, between March and July 2006.

2. Justin McGuirk, *Icon* magazine, Issue 037, July 2006, p. 91.

89 (previous page) and 90–91. **Ice Branch**, Swarovski (2005)

92–93. **Night Blossom**, Swarovski (2003)

94. **Night Blossom** detail, Swarovski (2003)   95. **Blossom Chandelier** detail, Swarovski (2002)

99. **Come Rain Come Shine**, multi-color, Artecnica with Coopa Roca (2004)

100. **Come Rain Come Shine**, white detail, Artecnica with Coopa Roca (2004)   101. **Come Rain Come Shine**, multi-color detail, Artecnica with Coopa Roca (2004)

102–103. **Come Rain Come Shine**, white, Artecnica with Coopa Roca (2004)

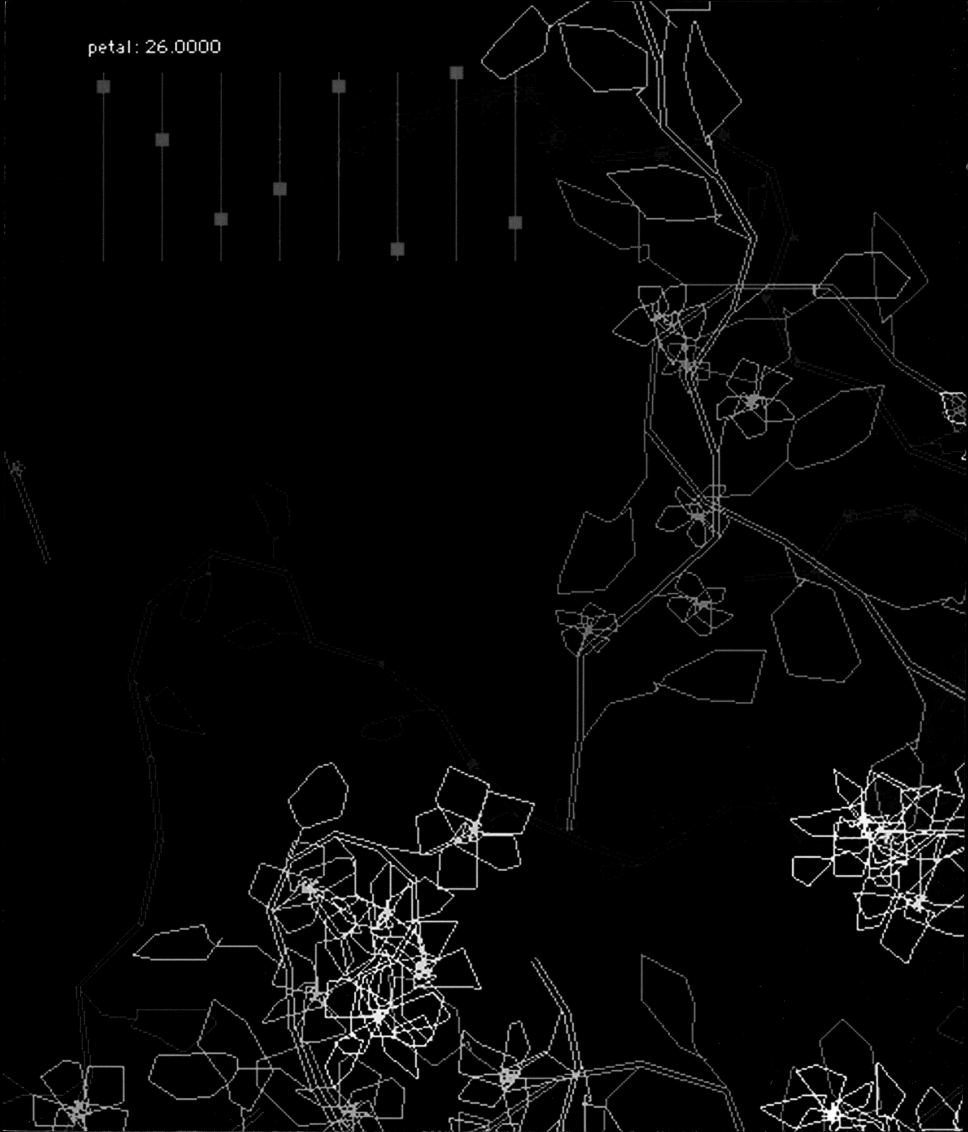

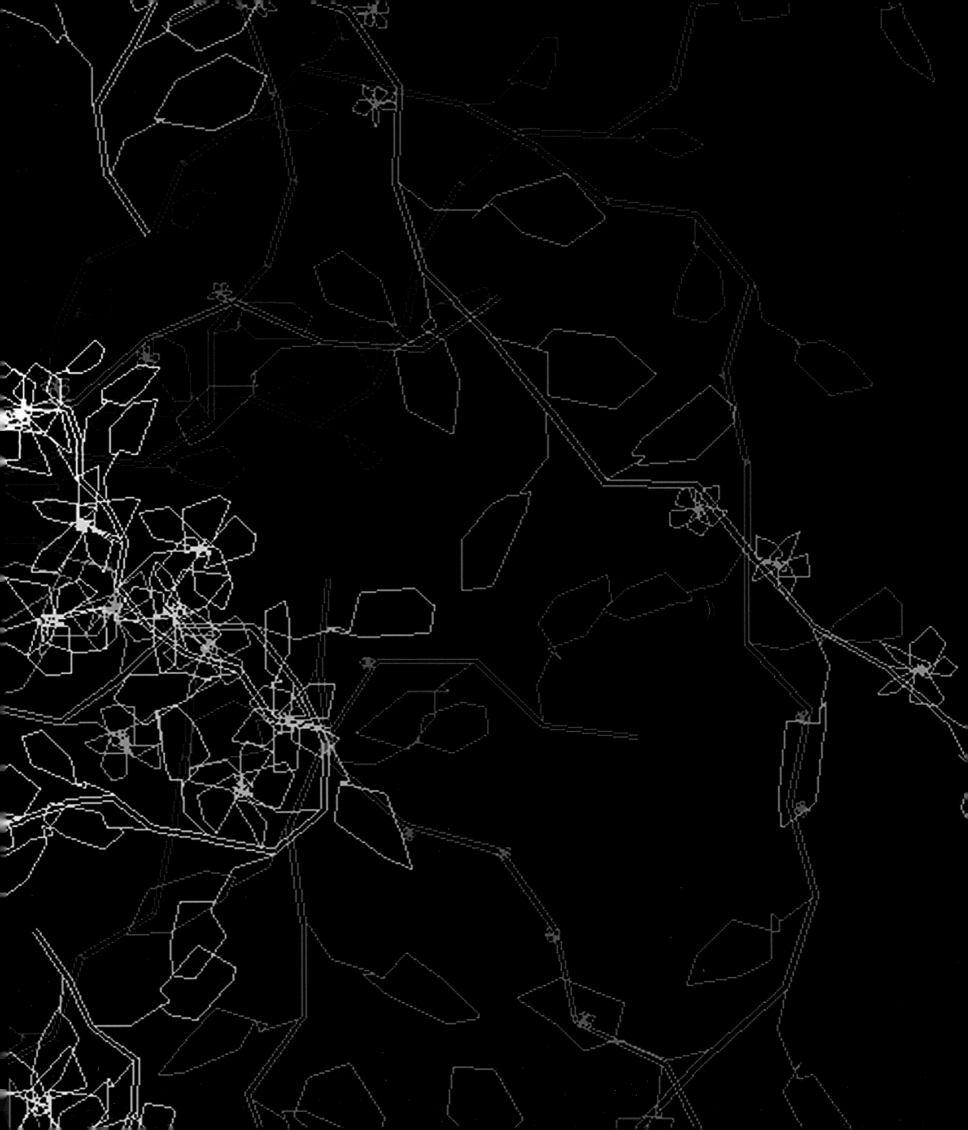

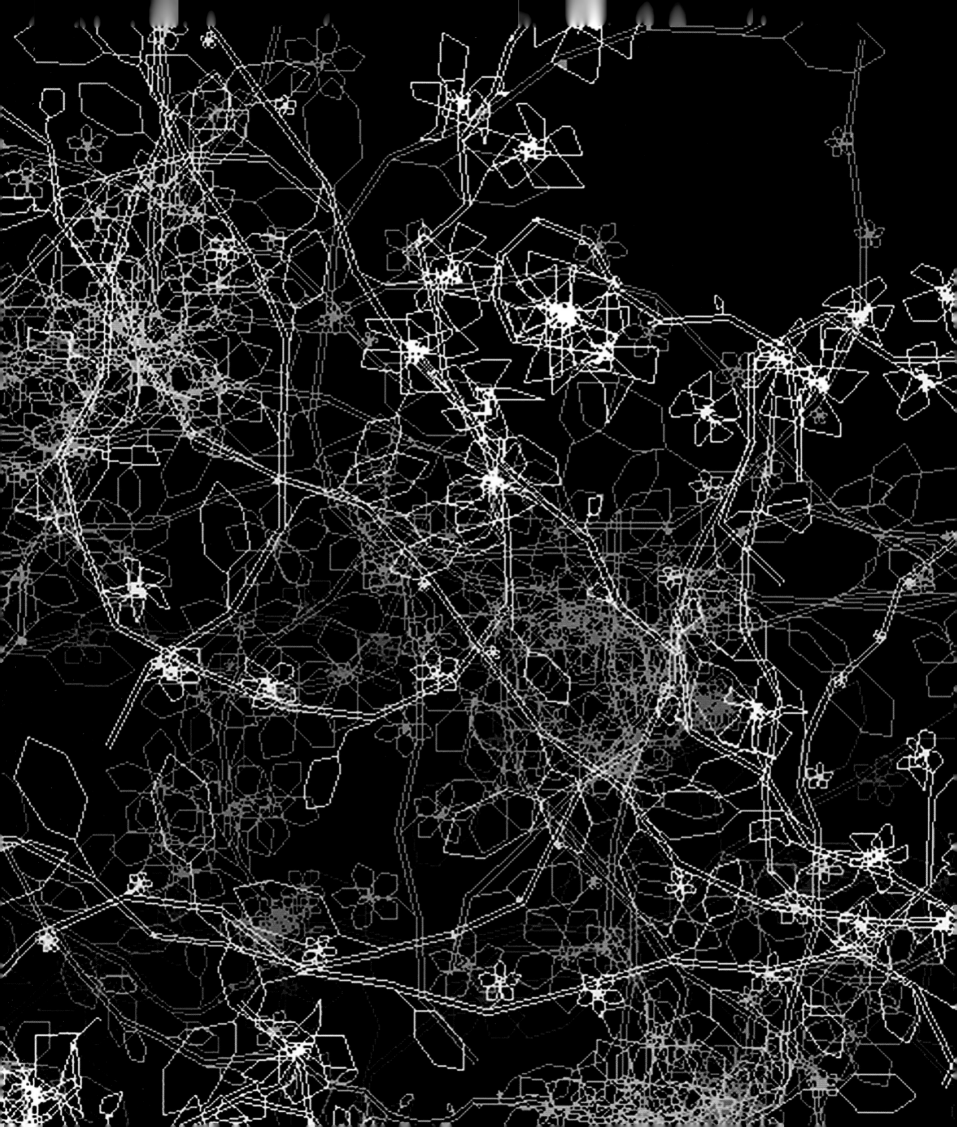

112–113 and 114–115 (previous). **Inflorescence** (2003) 116. **Inflorescence Vase** (2003) 117. **Nectar** (Inflorescence fabric), Kvadrat (2005)

Thinking & Doing

For Boontje the creation of products is a humanistic concern, combining nature and culture, the oldest and the latest materials and technologies, forms, functions and color combinations, and the aesthetics of ornament. How he combines all the elements is a kind of mental and physical bricolage, a collage of layers and assemblage of material elements, thoughts and intentions. "I am completely messy, completely random,"[1] Boontje says. He has a particular way of thinking and collecting, deep and wide, ranging through history and cultures and across disciplines, closely observing contemporary culture and researching the past, so that ideas when they come can seem strikingly complete. His friend Ben Panayi says this has been characteristic of his method throughout the years he has known him since their student days at the Royal College of Art: "I would have sketchbooks of drawings, he was able to just work it out in his head. The genius of being able to bystep one and two and go straight to three; that's just him."

The collaged design and production approach extends to the physical studio space. Paul Neale, director of Graphic Thought Facility, the designer of this book and friend, enthuses: "One of the things that I've become most excited about was when I visited the new studio in summer 2005 for the first time and saw the completely Tord way he dealt with the spaces, building this little Tord village, almost, of **Rough-and-Ready** p.25–32 architecture inside" (referring to the title of Boontje's first independent body of work nearly a decade ago, the products of which still furnish the studio space). Like a *caravanserai*, within the cavernous studio space is a series of workshop/computer design/office "rooms" out of light industrial materials, pinboard, chipboard, polystyrene, polycarbonates, populated with computers, mobiles, box files, fabric samples, jam jars full of paintbrushes, pencils, marker pens, wood samples, periodicals, catalogues, books, color swatches, crystals, outsize and tiny intricately cut paper models, drawings, cuttings from fashion magazines, engravings and images from books, and Boontje's own products in haphazard groups.

The materiality of the studio, as space and experience, embodies a physical act of communication. There is an affinity with choreography in the production of work, the criss-cross movement in the studio of Boontje and his staff, the bond of shared tacit knowledge, using CAD, fabricating in the workshops, experimenting, researching, phoning, discussing, packing and unpacking, cutting and shaping, welcoming visitors, stopping to eat a picnic lunch outside of pate, rye bread, herrings, salad, oranges. As for a music or theater director, there is the script, the score—the design—and there is the process of interpreting and realizing this in three-dimensions for an audience. In the studio, Boontje provides hands-on vision and direction, but there are areas of independence, with Laure-Anne Maisse as administrator, Laure Grezard, Simon Reynaud and Rugiada Petrelli as designers/fabricators alongside one or two interns for short periods.

121

a.

b.

Locating production in France is not an issue. As Panayi says: "It's not important where you live, but where you present your work." Having work in fairs such as the annual Milan Salone de Mobile or periodicals like *Domus* is what matters. But the studio isn't just a private place, it is an interface with clients and the media. The studio is an important extension of the self and the design agenda. When Authentics, the German product manufacturers, thought about working with Boontje, it was the owner-directors' visit to the London studio that clinched it. When journalists visited the studio in France for a launch of his Kvadrat fabric collection, they were captivated by the sheer exuberance of the work in the festive context Boontje had created for it and recognized that, for him, the practice of design and the practice of everyday life are unified.

The designer's progress towards professional recognition began, however, without a studio in the mid 1990s as a solo, self-generated activity in corners of his wife Emma's south London glass studio and rented flat. In the evenings he would say to Emma: "I've had an idea." The idea for **tranSglass**^{p.33–35} started straightforwardly in early 1997 because Emma had the glassmaking equipment for her own burgeoning career as an artist and the raw material of wine bottles was abundant in London's recycling units. He started working in close partnership with Emma on both design and production. But in the making Emma was proficient, while Boontje more than once cut his hands on the machinery and was rushed to the hospital, Panayi stepping in to help maintain production.

They were delighted that shops such as Tom Dixon's Space in Notting Hill took it on and others followed, fueled by eloquent publicity photographs, which Boontje knew were vital tools of promotion. His display of tranSglass at London's new fair, 100% Design, was also a success. Production steeped up into the hundreds, and they took a neighboring unit in Rushworth Street for a year and then sought to achieve production on an industrial scale. This was eventually secured only in 2005, when the American company Artecnica's *Design with Conscience* program embraced the ethical and educational design ambitions Boontje has always had as part of his work.

Enrico Bressan, Artecnica's co-founder/director, and Boontje worked together with the help of the non-profit Aid to Artisans organization to train fourteen young people in Guatemala in the production of tranSglass, while others are now relieved of "living on rubbish dumps," Boontje explains, by contributing the raw materials for tranSglass, "able to collect the bottles from hotels and bars" to eke out a living. The success of the project is held up as a self-sustaining product design model worldwide, supporting a local community to make a design classic, now in the permanent collection of the Museum of Modern Art in New York.

For the same combination of humanitarian, artisanal and environmental reasons, Boontje and Bressan are involved in the Coopa Roca project in Rio de Janeiro's shantytown district of Rocinha. Started a generation ago by Maria Teresa Leal, some 150 women use traditional craft skills to make products from home created by contemporary product and fashion designers. Following an

c.

d.

e.

f.

a. The studio, 2006; *right to left:*
Simon Reynaud, Tord, Laure
Grezard.

b. The studio, 2006; *right to left:*
Rugiada Petrelli and Laure-Anne
Maisse.

c. Bottle Mountain in Dagenham
where material was collected.

d, e. Transglass production in
Guatemala City.

f. Transglass installation at
Stealing Beauty, ICA, 1999.

inspired initiative in 2004 with Coopa Roca by Emily Campbell, Design Director of the British Council, Boontje created the startling flower-trailing, crocheted chandeliers **Come Rain Come Shine** p. 99–103, now, as with tranSglass, supported in their manufacture and distributed by Artecnica.

These principles of self-reliance and empowerment through the skills and pleasure of making things underpinned Boontje's own first independent collection of furniture, pragmatically entitled Rough-and-Ready. This evolved in 1998 as a conceptual extension of his provisional domestic environment. (As Emma says: "we never bought any furniture until Evie was born," finding all their needs from skips and their own constructions). The wood was simple plywood and the epiphany for the collection was the raindrops on the polythene sheeting found in the street, which became part of the shelving unit and lights, evoking Boontje's mantra: "The idea of beauty in everything." The Rough-and-Ready collection, iconically photographed by Boontje in a nightime rain-soaked London back street, a kind of *Bladerunner* atmosphere, narrated in tableau form the revolt from excess, the rethink on values in the 1990s.

Boontje lists the inventory of the collection: "four tables, two with cement board, one cardboard, one conti board, three or four lights, a cabinet, benches and shelving." The only modification Boontje made was to the chair, substituting plastic strapping—"even more rubbishy"—for the black ducting tape, which tended to peel off the blanket "upholstery," a readymade found in an army surplus store. None of it was for sale, since materials, method, form, and presentation were a democratizing "experiment, a notion," not a commodity. The point was to be a producer, not a consumer. Rough-and-Ready put down a cultural marker and curators began to contextualize the work in key exhibitions (discussed in the next section of this book). Production and meaning were symbiotic: at each exhibition you could take away a plan to make the

a. Rough-and-Ready photographed in the street, London 1998.

b. Coopa Roca in Rio de Janeiro.

c. Advertising still from Alexander McQueen of Boontje's eyewear.

a.

b.

blanket chair. To date, 35,000 people have taken away the plan, with its symbolic message of the self-reliant simple life.

Alongside this early self-generated production, in 1998 Boontje had begun an association with Alexander McQueen to design eyewear and watches for the accessories strand of the fashion designer's output. "We got on very well, very naturally" says Boontje, who was inspired by McQueen's fashion show videos, noticing, "the really strong makeup round the eyes and stylizing that and using that as a lens shape and through that creating completely new shapes." Facial expression can be shaped by eyewear, so the McQueen look was "sharper and a little bit more aggressive," not ornamental at all. A watchstrap with square links should look "sharper and minimal." Trino Verkade, now Creative Coordinator and McQueen's first assistant from the early 90s start ("when he was a hot new designer but still quite underground"), appreciates that Boontje was "pushing it from a technology and materials point of view, something we didn't have knowledge of so much," such as the proposal to use cooling ceramic for the eyewear sidebars, which they tried but could not be done. (Later "Donna Karan managed it," Boontje smiles ruefully.)

Referring to McQueen by the name used by friends, Verkade says "Tord's Panda Eye was one of Lee's favorite ever glasses; it became quite iconic in Japan." In the production process McQueen is in control, balancing the collection—"too commercial, too wearable, needs more sharpness," Verkade comments, McQueen is "very emotional" and responds incisively: "everything's quick, everything's a gut reaction: 'is that me, do I like it?' If he likes it, then it's fine."

McQueen and Boontje have a shared interest in spectacular display and collaborated on a crystal-laden Christmas tree for the Victoria and Albert

124

c.

Museum in 2003, now in Swarovski's Crystal World in Austria. Two years later, McQueen showcased everything Boontje had done in the Carousel show in his store at the Milan fair in 2005, a hugely successful collaboration. Working with McQueen reinforced the idea of a personal design language. Boontje recognized that you can do all kinds of production, not a house style, and a loyal following develops. Both Boontje and McQueen, Verkade says, "have this appreciation of modernity, pushing boundaries. You've got to stick to your aesthetic guns. If you continually move, you can't entice people into your world. You have to stand for something and you can only stand for what you believe in. It's not about a silhouette. It's about an attitude."

Boontje emphasized such thoughts with his Wednesday collection, launched in January 2001. He had received a commission with an open brief from Andree Cooke, now with Arts Council England and at that time curating the British Council's Window Gallery, literally nine huge window spaces fronting a busy main street in Prague, an unusual international context. This was a vital solo show for Boontje, as it had been for others commissioned by Cooke, such as Hussein Chalayan, Dunne&Raby, Philip Treacy, and Tomato. By his own admission, the birth of Evie in 2000 made Boontje think even more emphatically: "What do I want, how do I want to live. I really felt I had to make the next step in my work. I carefully formulated a new direction, a new thinking."

Boontje recounts the process: "Three things happened at the same time. I was looking at museums like the V&A; I was also looking at technology, how to use technology, and I decided to make things as well, thinking through making. I took a Rough-and-Ready chair and I embroidered a crow on it, I still have it in the studio. Not perfect embroidery; it had to look like it was made by a real person, not in a factory. They were not really products; experiments, thoughts. There was never a Wednesday logo because it didn't feel right to brand it."

"I would make models in cardboard. The more I could visualize these things before I would make them, the more I could justify the making itself, because it took a lot of time to make these pieces. I would use a corner of Emma's workshop." The sewing was a personal pleasure for Boontje, done freehand, the materials again chosen for their vernacular connotations. Clothing the chairs added a tender warmth of personality. The glassware, from Boontje's designs, was handblown by Simon Moore, thick heavy vases with perforated decoration. Moore was impressed by Boontje's level of interest in the glass techniques undertaken in Moore's studio and by Boontje's ingenious idea of the nailboard with horse and bunny to create the decoration on the molten glass (later adapted for a collection from Salviati and from Dartington Glass, where Moore was then Design Director).

Boontje chose metal instead of wood for the table because "maybe wood was too old-fashioned." The resulting perforated metal table and cabinet with

125

a.

b.

poured resin produced an aesthetic of both spontaneity and risk, of beauty and decay, material deconstructed and dematerialized. Boontje was inspired by the operation of chance as a procedure in the paintings of Willem de Kooning and furniture of Gaetano Pesce and by the proportions and form of William Morris's cabinet. Cooke describes the appeal as "something which appears to be very personal," which offered "a new approach to materials" and was "part of a larger movement towards individualizing things" within a context of the ordinary and the everyday. "Although they were products they weren't products," Cooke says. "He was incredibly excited to have the solo show and in a new context. In general his whole life was blossoming. I just thought: this will make his career." She was right.

The Wednesday collection, seminally, included the **Wednesday Light** p.57–58, the first version of a light later globally industrialized and made famous as Habitat's **Garland** p.59–62 light and more recent versions from Artecnica. The idea originated as a drawing on paper and a paper modeling of a garland round his daughter Evie's bedroom light. Despite the apparent impracticality of his garland design's function and the cost of producing what in effect were a limited edition of prototypes, Boontje went ahead and GTF designed the graphically ingenious packaging. For Boontje, "it was the first time I had got a factory to do something. Twelve were made originally. I had no idea it would be successful."

Tom Dixon, renowned designer and in 1998 Design Director of Habitat, tells the story of how he brought the Wednesday light to a mass market, achieving the rare status of a design classic loved by all ages ("my *mum* loves it," Dixon enthuses). "I'd seen the Wednesday light. I thought this is the simplest and cleverest thing I've seen for a long time. Often with the simplest ideas you can miss it." Dixon wasn't fazed by the flowers: "I've even done an ikebana course once in Japan just for fun, so I was all for flowers. I've always been bored by what's happening now and always wanting what's next, so it did seem right, the flower thing. But trying to stress the importance of something so decorative in Habitat at the time was quite tough. Nobody saw the significance of the thing."

Some design and material changes were made to differentiate it from Boontje's own limited edition, which he had had to price at £150 each to cover his costs. Dixon says: "For me it was a bit of a mission. I knew the price of acid-etched brass and the Garland launched at £15. We underestimated quite massively, which also strangely worked to our benefit. We went out of stock immediately. It was the first real mass hit I'd had. I'd got it in the catalogue, the shop window, the press motivated, working all the way through. There were waiting lists, queueing. Hundreds of thousands were sold. It was the million-pound item, which is the holy grail. I wasn't that surprised frankly, but surprised I'd managed to convince anybody, because it was very different."

"It's got a fashion edge, it's disposable, giftable, flatpack. It has all of the qualities a Habitat product should have. I spent the next year battling with various departments to get more Tord products and ended up buying the curtain from Artecnica for our Christmas window. It still makes me feel slightly sick. I

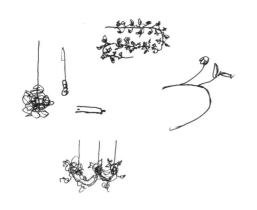

c.

e.

d.

a. Nailboard for making patterns in hot glass.

b. Paper bedroom light for Evelyn, 2000.

c. First sketch for the Wednesday Light, 1999.

d. Packaging for Wednesday Light, designed by Graphic Thought Facility.

e. Creating the package artwork in a darkroom by exposing a cube of photographic paper wrapped in the garland.

regret that Habitat didn't consider wholesale or internet shopping," Dixon says. "All too many people miss success. If Habitat had a part in that, then I'm happy."

Habitat's mass production of the Garland light began to universalize Boontje's impact. It is lights that have spearheaded Boontje's reputation. Following Garland, the crystal **Blossom**p.95–97 chandelier for Swarovski, inspired by a frozen cherry branch, has been collected by museums worldwide, by Elton John and a member of Metallica. The commission came from Nadja Swarovski, trained art historian, gemologist, and young Design Director in the fifth generation of the venerable Austrian family of crystal manufacturers. Her aim is to put contemporary design on the firm's creative and business agenda, led by new technology. Understandably passionate about crystals, Swarovski says: "The only thing I can vouch for is they make people happy. I've seen two-year-olds and 92-year-olds just fascinated with them. The crystal is a lantern and reflects light and light subconsciously to us means life. So if you have a material that transforms light, let's use it."

Swarovski had initiated a new design direction for the firm by commissioning leading fashion designers and jewellers to use crystals in innovative ways in their work, to spectacular effect. She then surveyed the chandelier manufacturers, to whom her company had supplied crystals for over a century for clients such as Queen Victoria. She concluded, "they were doing *nothing* to introduce new designs so we took it up ourselves. Let's raise the bar here." In her mission "to reinvent the chandelier" Swarovski acknowledges that it "was hard to get the designers on board" because of the reputation of the company for rather sentimental crystal ornaments, "but Tord is one of those people who is so used to thinking out of the box. He was able to think beyond that and look at the individual component and think what could *he* create."

When they saw the Blossom chandelier, "we were blown *away*," Swarovski glows. "Tord went so beyond the brief that we had given him, so connected to nature, so modern, so beautiful, so powerful." The effect of the *Crystal Palace* exhibition at the Milan Salone de Mobile in 2002, which included ten designers, was immediate: "People came in from the street and fell totally silent." Chandelier manufacturers, hitherto complacent about the traditions of their market-

127

a.

b.

c.

d.

Winter Wonderland production:

a, b. Tord's brother Adri Edlund
welding and making a mountain.
c. Sledge under construction.
d. Laure and Claudine Grezard
gluing crystals.

place, started producing versions of the Blossom and Swarovski had to take legal action,'"raising the bar in terms of industrial ethics and design."

Swarovski continues: "We loved his product. We wanted it to be in the hands of everyone" and so different sizes of Blossom were produced and wall sconces and table top objects and a crystal wall tattoo, a crystal flower pattern you could apply directly to your wall. The appeal of his products, Swarovski believes, is because "he awakens the child within us, that's the power of his products. You feel comforted by them."

The glamour of crystals extends to some of the spectacles Boontje has been involved in for Swarovski, including Fashion Rocks in Monte Carlo in aid of the Prince's Trust in 2004 and a charity fashion gala in New York in 2006, for both of which he designed and produced crystal decorative schemes. Boontje recalls the fun of the French event—flown into Monte Carlo by helicopter with his family at night high over the Cote d'Azur—where, in the arena of his design, The Kills played while Prada showed their clothes; the high life "for a day." The more enduring spectacle created by Boontje is *Winter Wonderland* at the Swarovski gallery in Innsbruck, Austria, installed for a few years, and he was chosen because, Swarovski says, "he would be the one to add that magic, the one with the magical hand."

The idea Boontje developed was for a "whole evocative landscape" which you would walk through and discover, "as many elements as possible in that small space and also because I love stories and fairy tales, especially those reflecting a wintry situation." In the **Winter Wonderland** p. 232–237 installation, a cabinet's open doors reveal shoes, bags, clothes, jewelry — "I really wanted to get Dorothy's shoes in there," says Boontje, referring to an effort to get the shoes Judy Garland wore in the film of *The Wizard of Oz*. Elsewhere a boat is trapped in ice, echoing the start of Mary Shelley's novel, Frankenstein, or Ernest Shackleton's Antarctic odyssey, spending the winter marooned in an icescape, "which made a big impression on me," Boontje relates. The evocation of dramatic incident is everywhere. A sledge with a crystal rose steeped in snow, suggestive of the kingdom of Narnia, a wall of cut strips of mirror, a fractured image alluding to distorted beauty at the start of *The Snow Queen*. There is an abandoned tea party with animals and a cake, butterflies, blossom chandeliers evoking the coming of spring, tables, benches, glass and crystal, clouds of snowflakes and icicles at the stairs, "a really dramatic moment of entering." A whole tree played a part, found lying across the path in France. "We were told to remove it and it was just the perfect tree, we brought it back to the studio and cut it and painted it white, applied resin and crystals," Boontje explains. Then there is a sheepskin-covered chair, "like a polar bear."

In a high-risk strategy, the entire steel-fabricated wonderland was created without a model. "Straight off, drawn on the computer, then cut and bent and twisted. It came out so unexpected that you really cannot imagine how somebody could possibly have conceived of it—because—we didn't!" grins Boontje. "Five massive trucks transported it and eight people assembled it," working out the logistics to get the boat, floors, ceiling, architrave and tree in before the icicles on the staircase "with millimeters to spare." Throughout, Boontje remained characteristically "quite optimistic" of the outcome, and even in the studio he says, "for me it's stressful, but most of the time really enjoyable to do." As it took shape in Innsbruck, installers "stared with their mouths open. We knew it was a fantastic thing."

A collaborator on *Winter Wonderland* was computer programmer Andrew Allenson, who shares Boontje's interest in new technology and its potential to develop the language of design. Both having taught at the RCA (and inspired by Andrew Shoben), their collaboration goes back to 2002, when Boontje focused on the technology of wall decoration of a never-ending kind. The question he asked was how to create a continuous changing dialogue of an image, a new function. That was the idea for **Inflorescence**[p.112–119], Allenson says, to create something "without so much direction, so that the designer could relinquish control. This challenges the role of the designer because with this process you are not strictly designing it any more."

Coming from a design language and application, the idea was to evolve new industrial processes with the effect of painting continuous pictures without a brush. Boontje realized there were rules to creating work in this way and according to Allenson "defined the generative grammar for making the flowers and I adapted it and made the software," for example working out the variance of flower form over time and the change from one size to another. A new grammar of ornament, originated by computer scientists a decade before, was thus embellished and inflected by these designers of Inflorescence, first seen in Boontje's solo show at the Barrett Marsden Gallery, London in September 2002.

The idiom and realization fitted the language of Boontje's work. "Inflorescence has some similarity with fractals but we created an aesthetic that was distinct," Allenson says. In subsequent shows, *Happy Ever After*, for Moroso in Milan, 2004, and *Karakusa* for Shiseido, 2006, the language evolved in relation to the dye-cut hangings and curtains "fitting the mood of the space." For and for **Target**[p.226–231], Allenson created animations using Boontje's animal drawings and interactive snowflakes. Like Boontje, Allenson sees a relationship between craft and technology: "Architects and designers can get bogged down in professional management and policy. Tord shows you can be more concerned with process and integrity and self-belief. I've always thought there is a similarity between craft and software. The production process is the same because you don't have to send it out to be produced... In the future, I would like to take Inflorescence forward as a software product, literally creating a continuous spectacle in and of itself."

Given Boontje's enduring personal interest and commitment to art and technology, and to environmental and ethical concerns, it is not surprising that Artecnica, discussed earlier in connection with tranSglass and Coopa Roca, has been an important client. The marriage between art and technology is evident in the company's name, in all its products and in the respective art and engineer/designer/architect backgrounds of its founder-directors, Italian-born Enrico Bressan and his wife, Tahmineh Javanbakht. Originally the sole designers for their company, the owners now work with international designers and with eco-conscious manufacturers and cooperatives in Brazil, China, Europe and South Africa to produce a range of home accessories and lighting, games, and stationery.

"We had been following Tord's work for several years before we contacted him," says Bressan. "The Wednesday light was the most visible of his works, showing the ornamental and aesthetic side. Once that element was in focus, my wife said: 'I'm just going to go ahead and send him an email.' It's not often that we find a designer so in tune and with so much integrity. He is extremely versatile and flexible and has commercial awareness. I think it's natural talent—you have an interest in why products and designs work and you have a good analytical capacity." Bressan continues: "Tord said that as a father narrating stories he started to realize, 'I'm narrating fairy tales to a child and no one narrates fairy tales to adults.' He starts to realize those things at a very conceptual level... gaining energy from that type of thought."

Bressan travelled to China to look at paper producers and resolved to create "very smart products by creating a lot with a little." The specification to Boontje was to focus on lighting made of paper, because Artecnica had already successfully marketed the Bloom card and Boontje's own design of a **Fairy Tail** p. 137 greeting card. Boontje's **Midsummer Light** p. 110–111, cut out like a double-layered shawl, "came to us as a fully-formed design." Boontje first used standard paper, then found a supplier for the flexible and more waterproof Tyvek, which he had always liked in the Federal Express packaging.

Boontje describes his creative process for the Midsummer Light: "I thought that you could cut paper so that it could become like lace, and if it was centered it could drape like a fabric, and from that came the Midsummer Light. The best way to develop it was to just cut the paper, drape it, look at it, change it, cut another one, and we probably made twenty different models in paper. People in the studio took it on as a kind of competition to see who could cut the quickest and the best; they had quite a lot of fun. Then when we had one that we liked, we scanned that into the computer. A very hands-on process." The die-cutting tool was made from the drawings "and we sent the final paper models as well." The amount of detail in the design was limited by what the tool could cut with very precise tolerances. Colors were chosen from Pantone swatches, varying in mood between bright, fresh, warm, and cool. The title, Midsummer Light, came to Boontje unbidden: "a lot of the names, they just come, apparently random." The **Until Dawn** p. 146–148 curtain followed.

The Midsummer Light was launched at the New York Gift Fair in January 2004. Bressan says: "We were quite sure we had a hit on our hands. The reaction was extremely good and some weeks later Moroso had it in the Salone de Mobile in Milan. It was the right product in the right place at the right time. It's hard to get all three and this did." The award of Best New Product at the New York Gift Fair confirmed its success.

The designer acknowledges that Artecnica has been "very important" for Studio Boontje, providing a secure income from royalties, opportunities to re-develop and distribute existing work, including the **Shadow Light** p. 106–109 and the Design with Conscience projects, alongside new products such as the polyester **Icarus** p. 104–105 light and **Thinking of You** p. 239–241, three metal vase covers, again using the favored metal-etching technique of the Garland light. It also meant that when Boontje got the call from Moroso in 2004, he had a ready-made source of existing products to use.

According to Patrizia Moroso, the doyenne design director of the Italian furniture manufacturers Moroso, the exhibition she commissioned from Boontje for the Milan Salone de Mobile in 2004 "made him famous." Just as Cooke felt her Wednesday commission "made his career," Moroso is right about the effect on Boontje of *Happy Ever After*. In melodious Italianate English, this is how she tells it:

Left to right Tahmineh Javanbakht and Enrico Bressan; Nadja Swarovski; Patrizia Moroso.

"The first time I saw something about Tord was in a magazine, maybe *Elle Deco*. I saw this page, it was a very small picture, not an article. I saw a special mood in this little chair. Sort of embroidery, staged by itself. Then I saw a nice chandelier." She realized it was the same person whose Garland light she had bought at Habitat in London. "I thought what clever ideas done with nothing, only with creativity. The chair was different from usual; the embroidery was by hand, little figures done by himself. Linen in different colors. It was the embroidery that I love. Not a nice perfect thing made by a girl. Very interesting. The designer was a guy, not common, not the normal meaning of a nice embroidery."

"The article had the phone number. I tore out the page and put it in my bag, sometimes looking and thinking. I kept looking and thinking, but I'm a little shy. I usually know someone, but I was an unknown person for him. I wanted to do something different in the Fair at Milano. So I phoned him one day because I decided he has to be the new designer of Moroso, not to produce one product but to do something in the showroom out of the Fair, not commercial. I asked him to display his way of thinking, absolutely free to do the work he wanted."

Needless to say, Boontje knew who Patrizia Moroso was and, despite the tight deadline he didn't hesitate: one week later he was in Milan talking about the project and went on to create, Moroso judges, "one of the best things we have done in Milan in our showroom." Bressan knew the Moroso company well and could provide quickly all the actual available products for the show, even though the Midsummer lights and Until Dawn curtains all required hand exfoliation from the etched and die-cut paper. The rest of *Happy Ever After*'s exhibits were designs prototyped by Moroso and other companies, including Kvadrat, and found chairs with mythical characters "dressed" in Boontje's studio. Besides furniture and objects, the sheer range of textural exuberance is suggested by part of the text from the show's poster-invitation of April 14, 2004, which promised, "fabric as exploration, fabric as couture, fabric as the bridge to an enchanted world. Organzas of silk in one ply, two ply and embroidered; cottons, cloths, felts, down-soft alcantara; plain seams, raw cuts, laser cuts, and weaves from the magic of memory."

Moroso says: "After the show he was really, really famous. It was magic, unexpected, completely new, stimulating, the border between design and art and other perceptions. With Tord a new period started, where everyone was feeling free to express the beauty of creativity."

To date, Boontje has created over fifteen products with Moroso and the request to describe her favorite piece reveals the relationship between design, craft and industry. "I got a phone call from London from Tord: 'Do you have some pieces of leather, it doesn't matter about the size?' I didn't know what he was going to do. Then he sent a picture and there were many pieces of black leather. My God, it's absolutely beautiful. You want to touch and to feel.

a.

b.

c.

d.

a. Development of Nest from a plaster model 1:10 scale.

b. Drawing the outlines on a block of soft foam.

c. Marino Moroso cuts the foam in the workshop.

d. Full size prototypes in soft and hard foam for testing comfort. After this stage, a 3D scan is made of the full size model, this data becomes a computer model for creating the tool. The two-dimensional artwork for the outside pattern is wrapped around the shape on the computer.

It's like an animal, like a sculpture, something that is moving." But this first **Witch Chair** p.178–179 was a one-off by Boontje and assistants in London and Moroso did not believe it could be industrially produced. "We found in the end the way to make it, a normal industrial product," Moroso says. "I was so proud and happy. There is satisfaction to see an industrial product. The idea to produce. We find the solution. We have to use two complete cows and a half to make it, a lot more leather than a sofa" (but fortunately using industrial offcuts). Finding a solution to industrialize an innovative product is the lifeblood for manufacturers as much as for designers and it is striking how it is the female members of distinguished family firms, like Patrizia Moroso and Nadja Swarovski, who are often taking a lead, something Boontje admires.

Moroso backs her own inclinations, choosing designers "who will give me something new." "Everyone likes Tord for the very extreme. Also now the smaller objects, the Corian table by Tord, using new techniques and technology. Corian was never decorated in that way before. Tord decided to work with that material. And the glass table surface, never seen before. It is the modernity of Tord to use technology and materials that are absolutely new and different, but to make the same luxury, magical effect that is done with expensive materials. The Swarovski chandelier, the same beauty can be found also in the Habitat Garland, the same effect. That is his way, to find the beauty also in the poor things. The plastic **Nest** p.159–161 chair, the surface is very new, a 3D in the skin of the object for the same price as an ordinary plastic chair."

Moroso concludes with a particular insight: "There are two sides to Tord. If people say what a nice man, I say, 'Have you never seen Tord angry? You don't know Tord at all!' Tord is a fantastic man of the woods, a dark side also. Tord can interpret a beautiful day or a terrible night and vice versa."

"The beauty also in poor things" that Moroso appreciates corresponds to Boontje's idea of "everyday ceramics, not Sunday best," which describes the poetic porcelain tableware series for Authentics, entitled **Table Stories** p.218–225, produced alongside his glassware and linen for the same company. The great tradition of storytelling on plates is evoked in red, blue and white colors and four stories, which can be mixed by the user to animate everyday encounters around eating. This flexible functionality and user interaction recalls the Rough-and-Ready chair and the Garland light. The Authentics project represented a move into the mass market of household goods, a further milestone in Boontje's career.

The Authentics company, based in Germany and known for the production of household and travel goods, received what the current owners, Elmar and Anna Flottoto, call "a new beginning" when they bought it in 2000. Although still producing what Boontje terms "mass market affordable products," Elmar Flottoto explains the new start was to provide "a platform for designers," to be a signature company. Design production and manufacture operates a loose network of information, whereby often designers themselves recommend to manufacturers others to watch for. In this case, Konstantin Grcic "told me to get in touch with Tord," Flototto recounts. "I went to see Tord in London. I saw his light for Habitat and I fell in love with his work in his studio." Why? "First of all, it's unique. And if you see it, it's full of love." Boontje recalls that when the Flottotos saw the Aladdin's cave of his London studio, full of materials, decorative motifs, people and color, for them "it opened up so many possibilities of how to do things differently." The timing was right for Authentics because, as Flottoto describes it, the economic situation was not good and "everybody was looking for something different, for something which makes you feel good."

The company has invested in a roster of individualistic voices, including several based in Britain such as BarberOsgerby and Shin and Tomoko Azumi. The aim is that each year, a new element, whether technical or aesthetic, is explored for the first time. With Boontje, the aesthetic approach was new for Authentics. The tableware used ancient methods, "We went to the roots of Chinese porcelain manufacture," says Flottoto, "but it was Boontje's own idea to have the four table stories and he devised the narrative alone. We never discussed the design. This is his work, his part. We discussed the function, the size of the plates and so on."

Discussing the reception of Boontje's products, Flottoto points out that Germany is notoriously conservative in the reception of innovative ideas in product design, perhaps ironically so since Germany in the 1920s, after the foundation of the Bauhaus, provided the heartbeat of contemporary design thinking. At the Frankfurt Messe in 2005, the key product fair in Europe, press reaction had, Flottoto remembers, "been immediate," but although buyers were intrigued by Boontje's work, representing something different from the usual Authentics idiom, the work "was going very, very slow." Then the subsequent showing in France, at the Maison d'Objets in Paris, "was a success, and it's becoming more and more accepted." In Japan, the reception of Table Stories is "very good" and internet shopping is the same.

A further mainstream product design commission has been with the Danish fabric manufacturers Kvadrat, guided by Anders Byriel, company director, who trained as an intellectual property lawyer and did not expect to run the family firm. Nevertheless, twelve years later, he is happily immersed, alive to the potential of broadening Kvadrat's contemporary design vocabulary and creating a retail presence.

Once again, the wheel of design connections turned. Byriel knew the work Boontje had done for Swarovski and knew Patrizia Moroso. "In February of the year Moroso commissioned the exhibition *Happy Ever After*, Patrizia introduced me to Tord's work. We contributed textiles for this event. Before the show in Milan we were very excited. We had been quite pure and minimal in our expression, so it was a big step for us." The change came naturally. "No, we were not seeking to change identity," Byriel laughs, but he could see that change was in the air and that textiles was a medium through which to express it. "During the 1990s and early 2000s, expression had been very reduced and minimal and Tord was a reaction to this movement. The reaction has to be original in a profound way and that's what Tord offered." The fact this expression was combined with a new technological edge provided the language for a new decade.

After the successful collaboration for *Happy Ever After* at Moroso, Byriel wanted to do something new, to maintain the momentum of interest, "like a second wave." He went to see Boontje in the Bakehouse studio in London and they brainstormed. "I call him a water tap. Like opening a water tap. Lots of designers do one, two, three ideas. He does so many. Tord has got a very exciting aesthetic edge and also a dark side. So he's on an edge, never pure romance; elements of tattoos; as a decorator very innovative, that's what makes him contemporary. We feel our contribution is very much working as a filter and molding the collection. Creating a logic and bringing him to a place where he would not otherwise be. Tord came with very strong and finished designs and it was easy to work with him."

Dorthe Helm, Design Coordinator, adds to the description of the process: "We had a short time to do the collection to a very, very high standard. We try always not to make any limits to begin with. We prefer designers just go mad, do what they want and cut down when we see production difficulties. We have the commercial point of view. It doesn't feel like a compromise." Helm perceived a more primordial content in some of the designs. "Very organic patterns with flowers, then mirrored in the middle of the design and again the other side; actually very erotic. Your mind takes you somewhere else than flowers."

The color arose from intensive discussions, "very much in a dialogue," says Byriel, since color is "one of our core competences." For some fabrics Boontje was seeking the pastel artifice of Boucher and Fragonard, but in others the dark tones of Francis Bacon and Rembrandt. The result is "uncommercial coloring," Byriel says, but paradoxically the more successful for it. "Aesthetics have been driving us, taking us somewhere new."

There were also technical innovations for Kvadrat: laser-cutting and digital printing, the former directly the result of the collaboration with Tord, the latter something which is extremely difficult to do with fabrics and which they had been working on for some time with Swiss and Japanese manufacturers in order to create a very clear expression in the fabrics. They additionally developed new materials, such as for Dreamer, a heavy woven material giving the sense of sails for a boat. For Kvadrat it was also the first time they printed on felt, finding pigments that didn't wear off.

Helm says, "For a long time we were looking at new techniques but didn't find the right patterns. Tord brought the right qualities. He couldn't just pick any fabric because there are very high standards of safety, and he couldn't do fine silk because we couldn't sell it to the offices market." For the printed wool, "we screen-printed small numbers, the wool fabrics supplied from England and the printing done in Switzerland. We didn't want to compromise. For example, on a three-meter (ten-foot) repeat we used two screens together, which is very complicated to do. The screen-printing was a huge amount of work and I hope this will be a new trend."

It took Kvadrat almost a year to produce the collection and using new suppliers meant everything had to be tested anew, sending batches separately to each country that would stock the work. Helm recounts with amusement the cultural relations inherent in global production: when they sent a CD of **Nectar**[p.117] to Japan for printing tests they heard nothing for days; eventually an email arrived from Japan saying they couldn't open the CD; the Japanese, for whom technical expertise is a matter of pride, had to admit then that they couldn't understand it because they had lost half the pixels in the design—"No, we said, that is how the design looked. Everybody was trying to be very polite!" Helm adds, "there were lots of safety tests to a very high standard, each using fifty meters (164 feet) of fabric. They decorated a whole room and set them on fire" until the required standard was reached.

Success can seem obvious with hindsight, but as Byriel recounts, "there

a.

b.

c.

d.

a–d. Design proposals for Target
store environment, Christmas 2006.

were people who predicted 'You are not going to sell one meter of this' because maybe it was too strong an expression." The launch took place in September 2005 in Amsterdam, using Moroso pieces and 1940s furniture from the private collection of the chairman of Kvadrat, which Boontje re-upholstered in his material. There was a further press launch in Boontje's studio in France. This was the designer's idea "to make it really personal," an event for which everything was handmade: "We dragged branches out of the forest, made all the stick chairs to drape the fabrics, to show it on furniture which wasn't furniture, then built all these long tables and benches. We used our Authentics tableware and tranSglass to drink and all these saucissons and wine; Emma cooked lentils and her mum helped." Lights and further fabrics were hung the length of the studio.

Byriel says: "Very fast the collection was totally sold out," a thousand meters (roughly three thousand feet) per color, and the collection received a Textiles and Contract Innovation award at the Cologne furniture fair in January 2006. "The full range of all the products is selling very well," Byriel says, "also the woolens. With Nectar you could expect it, but a lot were a surprise." In the aesthetic composition of the contemporary interior, Byriel suggests that "Tord is needed," citing minimalist interiors by, for example, Norman Foster or John Pawson. "The only thing that's needed is maybe a little bit Tord, like a bouquet of flowers. Tord is humanizing interiors."

Byriel concludes: "Critics have been changing their mind. Some of the hardliners were surrendering. People should watch out. There are lasting qualities in his design work...He's not a typical star; very down to earth, very, very gifted, such a nice guy. He's just here with the right thing at the right time." But Byriel acknowledges that "a lot of work is catching up, lookalike culture, which could reduce his own expression over time, so keep moving. I think Tord's designs will definitely dominate and be one of the key expressions of the 2000s and until we come into the 2010s. Our challenge with Tord is to keep moving, just stay excited. It's a long-term relationship."

A few months after the Kvadrat launch, in February 2006, Boontje finally had his first solo show in Japan, a country enthusiastically embracing his work. The *Karakusa* exhibition was held in Tokyo at the invitation of Shiseido, for whom the historical arabesque motif is an embodiment of their image and design spirit. The full range of Boontje's work was exhibited, but the innovation this time was the Petit Jardin bench which, says Boontje "was the first major one-off studio piece we've done in France and so we wanted it to have a French name."

The creation of this 120-kilogram (265 lb) steel bench started with a cardboard model, a favored approach of Boontje to the creation of new work: "We did a 1:1 scale drawing on the cardboard, cutting it out, stapling it together, taping it till we had the shape that we liked. We took it apart, we numbered all the pieces and then we took them apart, numbered up all the connections, photographed the flat pieces on the floor, and the photos we traced on the computer to get computer drawings for the laser cutting. We printed out the final production drawings at 1:10 scale to make the model, so that when the pieces came back from the factory we knew how to bend them and where to put what together. And that's it. So when flat metal arrives we know how to bend it, clamp it together, drill it." The success of this piece has encouraged Boontje to consider making an armchair version with a closed seat for added comfort. But for future editions, "I would never do anything really similar to this. I don't want to compete with myself."

A decade ago, Boontje started to develop his design identity through self-generated projects, and with Petit Jardin he has come full circle to consider this strategy again. But dominant are the mass manufacturing projects that have brought Boontje international recognition. By the end of 2006, Boontje had completed his largest project to date, for Target, an American retail conglomerate selling homeware, food and clothing, for whom Philippe Starck had previously worked. The project was planned with Louise-Anne Comeau, who has advised on similar projects with, for example, BarberOsgerby, Thomas Heatherwick and Swarovski Crystal Palace, helping to ensure projects are successfully realized.

"You can buy your whole life at Target," says Boontje, and for them he produced a complete scenario involving the design of over thirty-five different products, installations for nearly 1,500 stores, packaging and merchandising designs for all the Target 2006 Holiday products and the art direction of the print and television advertising campaigns. Despite "loads and loads of adjustments," intrinsic to huge manufacturing projects, Boontje found everyone "enormously supportive" from the top down, including marketing and product development teams and buyers. Although some of Boontje's designs had to be abandoned for reasons of complexity or unavailability of manufacturers or lack of shelf space—including the clothing range which would have been "new territory for us to go into," says Boontje—this has been Target's broadest commission ever for a designer, and "a huge investment" for all.

Over the last intensive decade of Boontje's career, the designer has engaged with multifarious materials, techniques, imagery and technologies and has investigated the potential of the forms and functions of things. The future modes of production could vary and extend, embracing also Boontje's first methodology of self-generated batch production. He might design a hotel or shop, produce and distribute a clothing range, develop new collaborations, perhaps relating to new technology and the moving image, respond to more projects in the public realm, such as one for a park in London's Canary Wharf for Christmas 2007. Sitting in the GTF studio, Neale reflects: "He is in a really interesting place at the moment, where he could go in so many different directions, developing the Tord languages on different canvases, working with interiors, his aptitude for theater, for creating spaces and installations. There are a lot of soft, warm, comforting components to his work, but still by varying degrees are the harder, darker elements and I, for one, am really pleased they're there."

1. All quoted speech throughout this section is from individual interviews with Martina Margetts, author of the text, between March and July 2006.

137 (previous page), **Fairy Tail**, Arcecnica (2003)　138–139, **Dondola**, Moroso (2004)

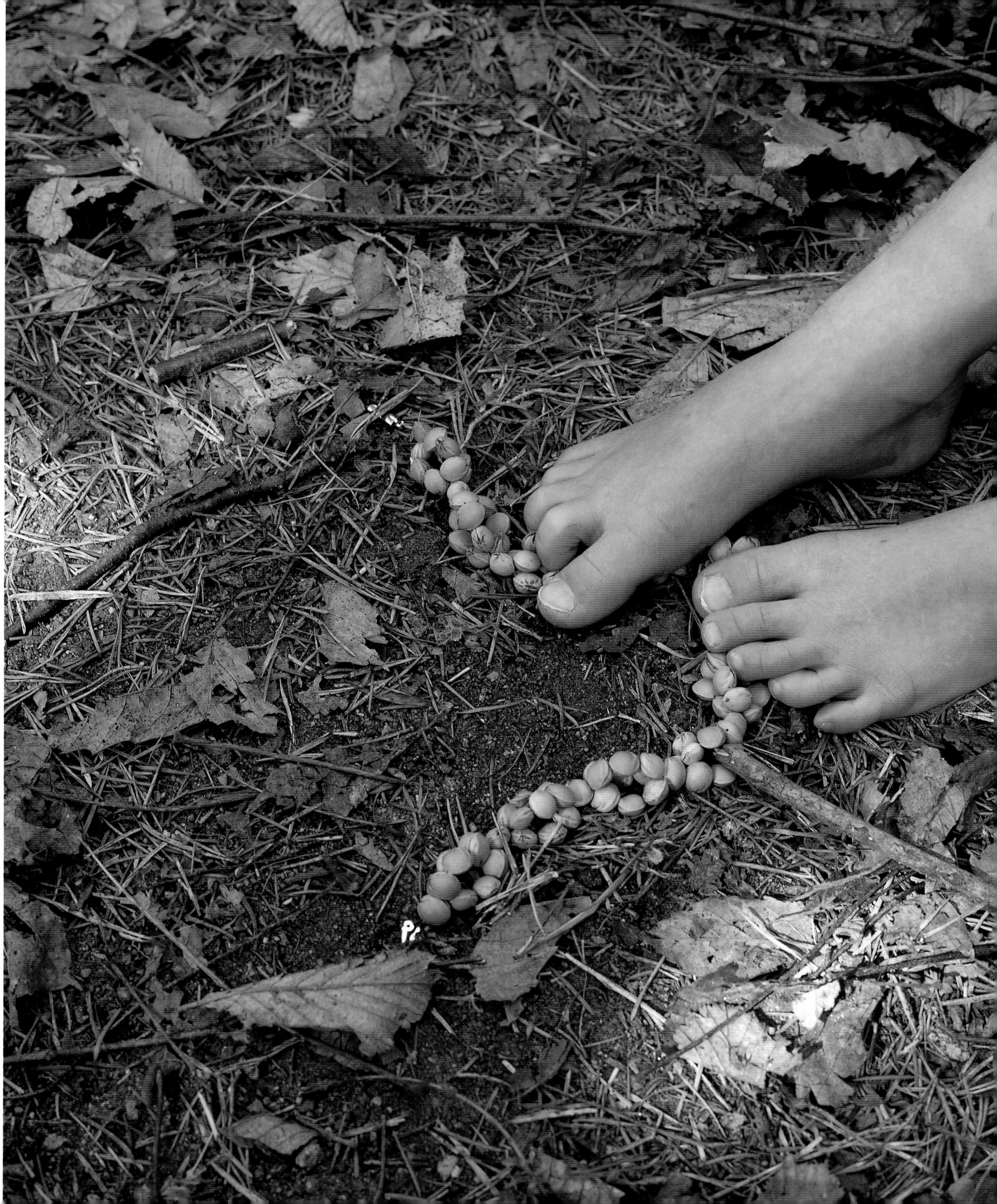

144. **Closer** detail, Moroso (2005)   145. **Cherry Pip Jewelry** (2005)

150–151. **Hello Lovely**, Moroso (2006)   152–153 (overleaf). **Bon Bon**, Moroso (2006)

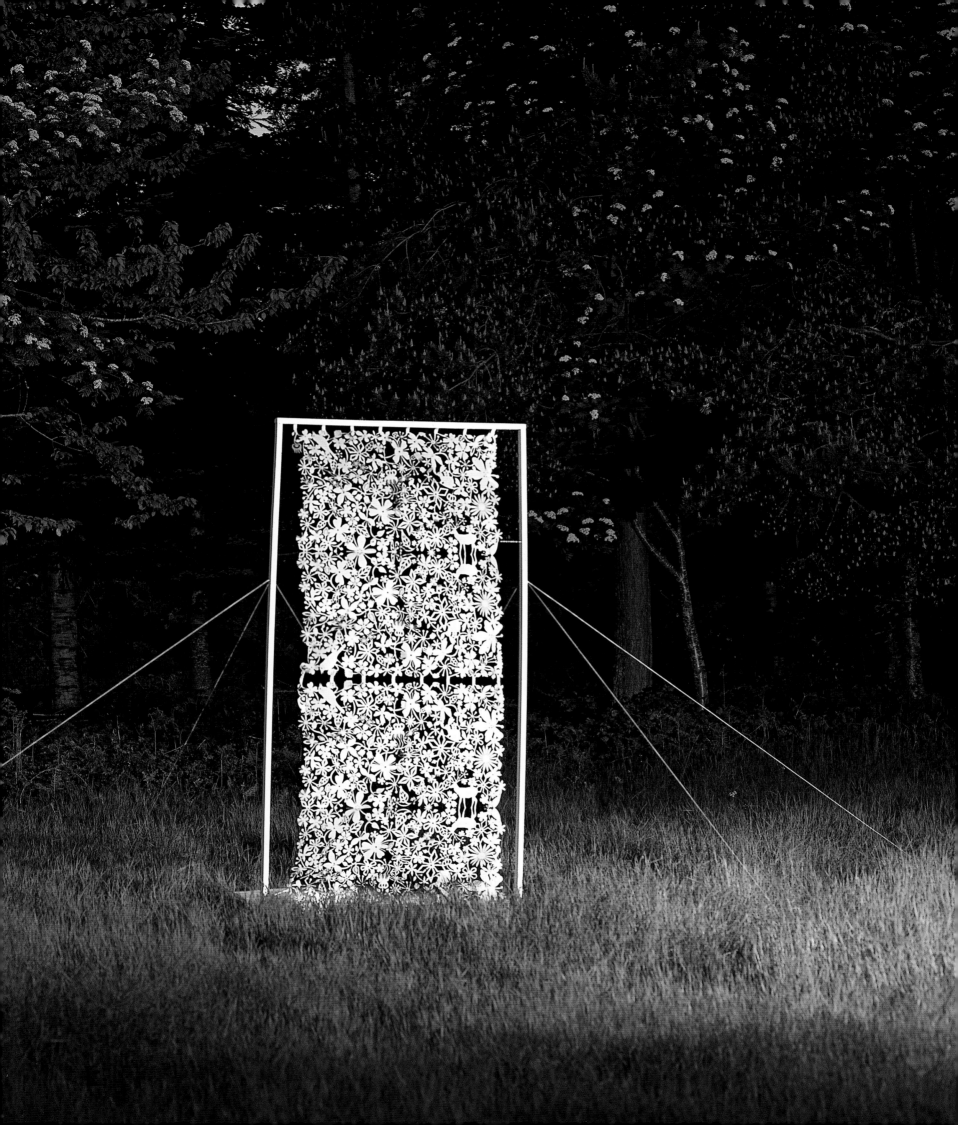

164–165. **Until Dawn** detail, Artecnica (2004)

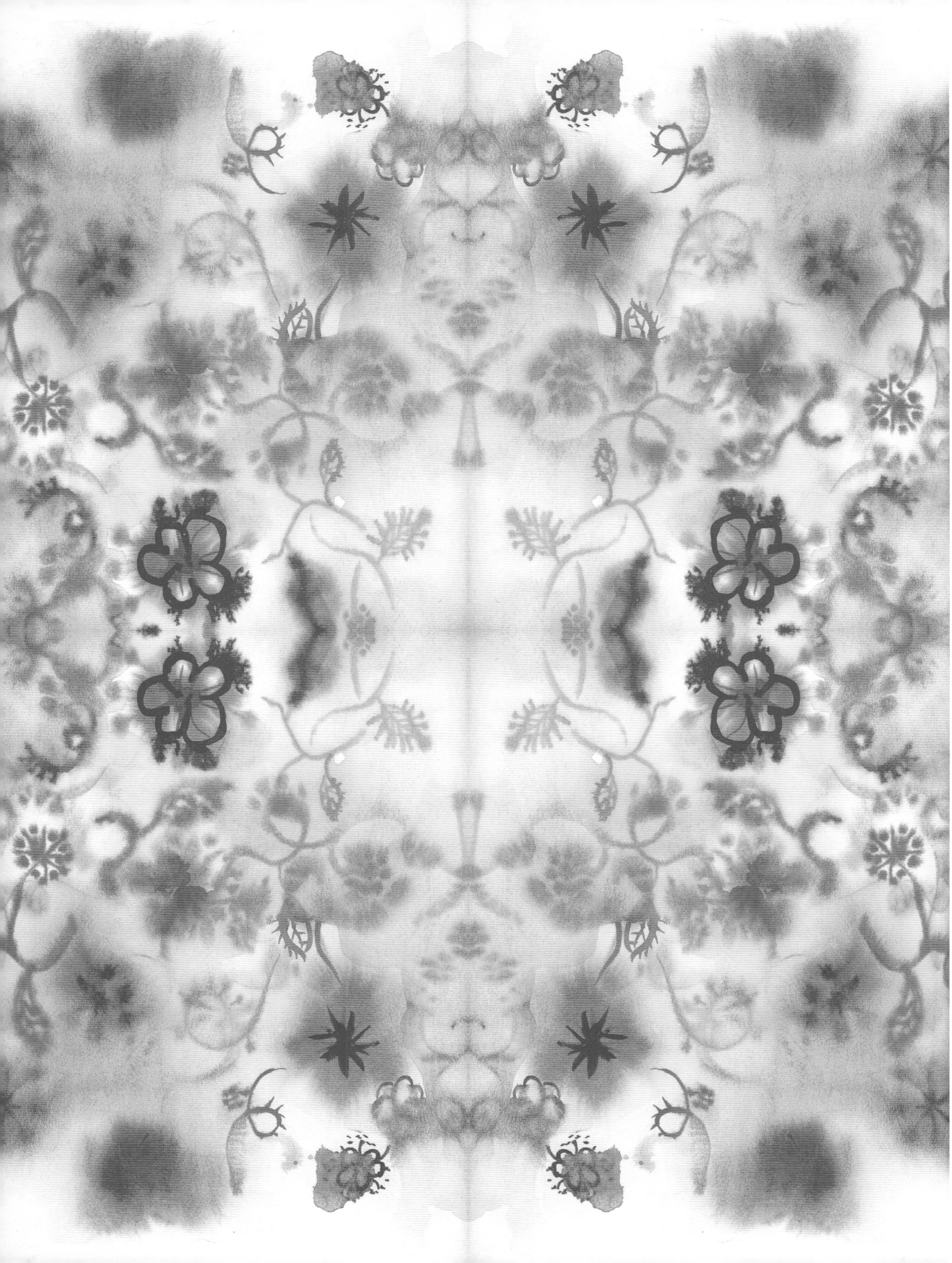

166–167. **Watercolor** (2004)

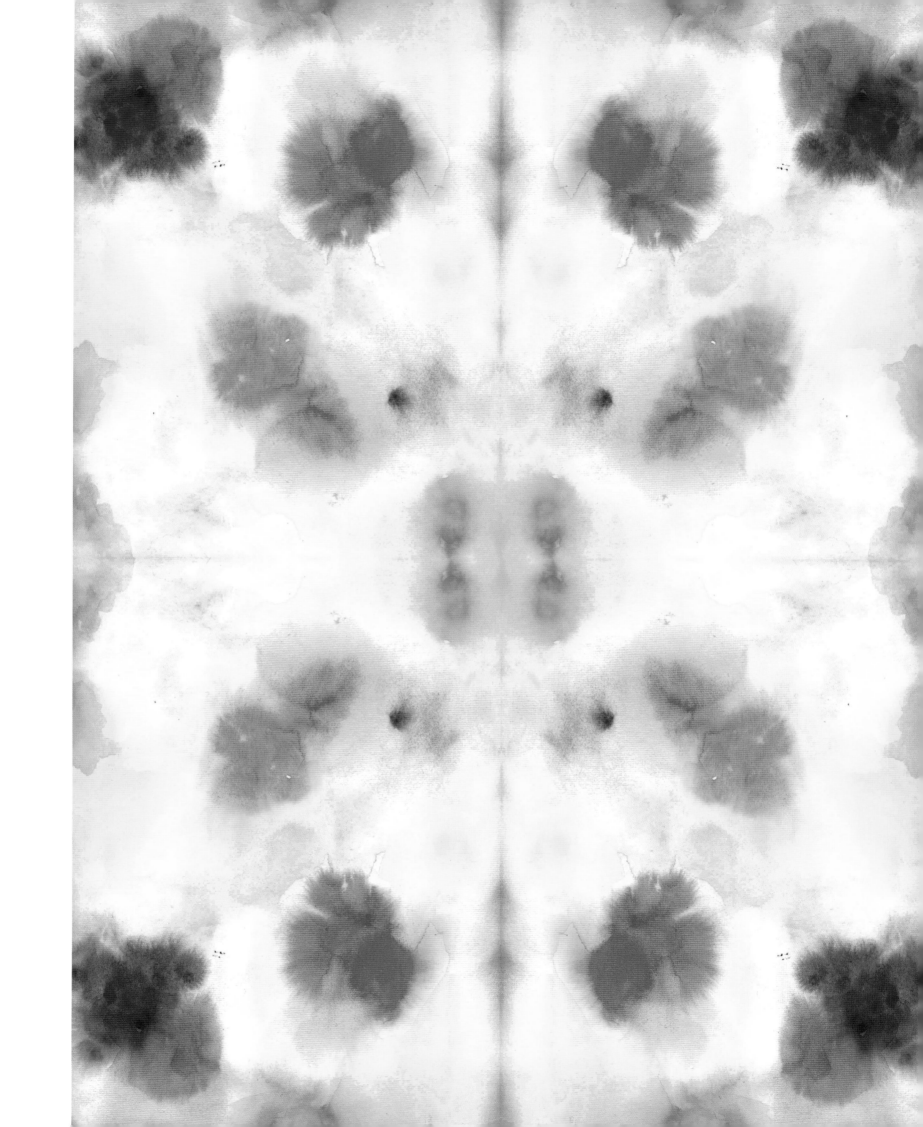

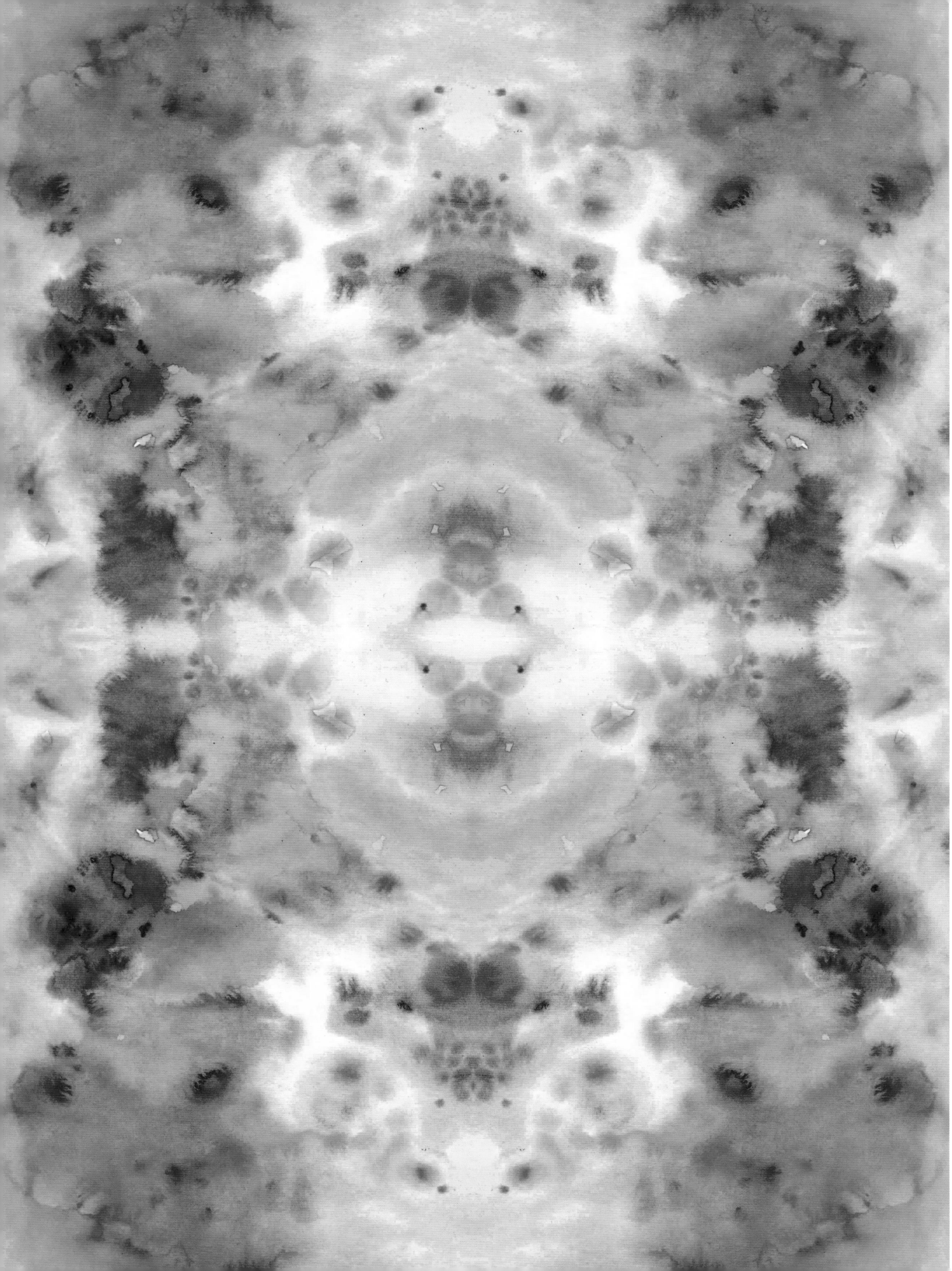

168–169. **Watercolor** (2004)

172–173. **Red Veil Chair** (2004)

176–177. **Princess Chair** (2004)   178–179 (overleaf). **Witch Chair** (2004)

180–181. **Forest Chair** (2005)

182–183 and 184 (overleaf). **Pirate Chair** (2004)

Light & Dark

In an intensive dozen years as a professional designer, Tord Boontje has secured a place in the design firmament. His decorative products have enlarged and altered the discourse of contemporary design. Ever broader waves of publicity during Boontje's career reflect the fact that his designs are both popular and widely available, now manufactured and distributed across North and South America, Asia, and Europe. The comment is frequently made that he is a designer producing certain products in the right place at the right time. This achievement is not by luck, but by design: his objects for use—made with unusual combinations of materials, technologies, and imagery—elicit fresh insights into how we want to live and what we value, re-enfranchising decoration, figuration, and hands-on process in the canon of iconic design. This new inflection of the design language has commanded attention and imitation. Paola Antonelli, a Curator of Architecture and Design at the Museum of Modern Art, New York, which institutionalized design as cultural artifact in the 1930s, says, "Tord made decoration industrial."[1] In countering minimalism, Anders Byriel, Director of the fabric manufacturers Kvadrat, says, "Tord has humanized interiors."[2] The context and influences that have informed these achievements are explored in this commentary.

For Boontje, the practice of design is a cultural activity and is unified with the practice of everyday life. It is, he says, "a vehicle to translate thoughts about the way the world is and what it should be."[3] He acknowledges that if design reveals meanings and thoughts about life it necessarily shows the light and dark side to indicate what he calls "the big subjects." Because of this intention the objects he produces transcend stylistic considerations to connect with history, with storytelling, with emotions and the importance of a free imagination. Boontje's work resonates because it represents a critical position: the countercultural stance of a social being who questions the orthodoxies and conventions of living; the romantic position of one who reconciles the influence of nature with the life of the city; the bricoleur who juxtaposes found materials and objects with new technological experiments, moving back and forth between historical reference and space-age temporality. Boontje is avowedly a product designer, he says, but as an amalgamation of many things: "caring socialist, environmentalist, poet, philosopher, illustrator, storyteller, colorist, material nerd, technological person, sculptor, entertainer, inventor."

The inchoate process of synthesizing thoughts to arrive at designs for a family of products is reflected in the myriad sources he collects. Here is an anecdote of how I first recognized his methods: It is midnight in Boontje's home in the verdant countryside an hour south of Lyons. The velvet sky is full of starry galaxies and all the woodland trees and the cows in the neighboring meadows are still. Inside, the logs are burning low and we are standing at the homemade

185

a. Artwork for Prince fabric showing one full repeat.

b. *The Magdalen Reading* by Rogier van der Weyden, from before 1438 Fragment cut from a larger altar piece, Oil on mahogany transferred from another panel 62.2 × 54.4 cm. © The National Gallery, London.

a.

dining table with a bulging A4-size book on it marked 'Wednesday.' Dozens of pages make up the scrapbook of thoughts and inspirational pictures, material possibilities and sketches of ideas for the Wednesday collection of 2001, which set Boontje on the path to international recognition. The book already has an historic quality and, in the sepulchral silence of the night, it is somehow magical to review its contents, for here is some of the raw material with which Boontje performs his own special kind of alchemy in the world of design.

The pages reveal Hungarian wooden churches, antiquarian botanical drawings, the Gothic tracery of an Oxford library ceiling, bamboo samples, Swedish folk art, Rem Koolhaas and John Pawson architecture, photographs of leaves and flowers, metal samples of photo-etching, Santa Maria Miracoli in Venice, the "favorite church" of Boontje and his wife Emma, the first pencil-drawn garland formation of the Wednesday light, and then, the painting of *The Magdalen Reading* by Rogier van der Weyden: a spiritual yet domestic scene, the busy folds of drapery, symbolic objects and colors, pellucid light and distant landscape, restrained furnishings and linear composition bearing the hallmarks of fifteenth-century Netherlandish painting.[4]

What Boontje says about this painting is a key to how he views the world: "I looked at this a lot with the Wednesday collection; the feeling of this had a lot to do with it. It's very domestic, it's really, really homely. When I was at college, I remember other students saying to me, 'your work is always so un-cozy.' This was the first time I wanted to create something warm in my work. I spent a lot of time at home as a family after the birth of Evie. My idea of home is not living in a white box. Something like a nest. From childhood I knew about the concept of a home."

Although Boontje was trained in Bauhaus principles and respects the classics of Modernist architecture and design, his idea of home is a place of spontaneity and informality, of warm-hearted disorder, where connections can be made and remade. Harmony is created by juxtaposition, not formal unity. In the large beamed and quarry-tiled living-room of the Boontje home, an ancient farmhouse with exposed stone walls and 1970s additions, there are Ron Arad and Shin & Tomoko Azumi production chairs, and Boontje's own **Midsummer** p. 110–111 and **Blossom** p. 95–97 lights, and his Kvadrat Prince blue curtains alongside IKEA's standard Billy shelving, and two Hella Jongerius vases, with a sheepskin

b.

rug and flatscreen Samsung television flanked by two brocade armchairs. There are books and an assortment of recycled jam jars and tranSglass vases filled with wild flowers and grasses collected by Evie.

   Here is the spectacle of the everyday, a place of intimacy and communality, of the mundane with the exotic—as Boontje says of his tableware for Authentics, "for everyday not Sunday best." It is an embodiment of Bachelard and Heidegger's ideas about dwelling and Freud's discussion of *das Unheimliche*,[5] 'the unhomely' or uncanny, the sensation which, according to Freud, is evoked when something which ought to have remained hidden has come to light.[6] The suggestion is that we project our unsettled view of the world onto things, but that things themselves can unsettle us by turn. Boontje's designs can give pleasure and comfort, but can also disturb. In his Kvadrat fabrics, for example, **Pressed Flowers**[p. 207–208] embodies softness, transparency and light, whereas Prince and the **Wednesday Light**[p. 58], (the forerunner of the Garland Light), with their thorny, sharp elements, echo the ensnaring and pricking of the innocent in fairy tales, a key source of inspiration for Boontje. (When I asked the designer Julie Mathias, a former student of Boontje what flower he might be, she had said "a rose," just as Patrizia Moroso had said he could interpret "a beautiful day and a terrible night," a quixotic character expressed through such works as his **Witch Chair**[p. 178–179] and vases for Moroso and black Come Rain Come Shine crocheted chandelier for Artecnica).

   The juxtaposition in Boontje's designs of cozy and un-cozy is reflected in his appreciation of both Surrealist and nineteenth-century culture. Within the

a.

a. Mural painted on a wall of the
Moss Gallery for *The End* installation.

b. Drawing of Wednesday Cabinet,
2000.

pages of Christopher Reed's now standard book, which re-enfranchised the domestic realm in Modernism's reductive agenda, the Surrealists rebel against the dogmatic rationalism of modernist architecture as "the complete negation of the image of dwelling," and view functionalism as "the most unhappy dream of the collective unconscious."[7] The idea that narrative, dream-filled, paradoxical, emotionally-charged content and a time-warped form blurring man, machine, home, self, art and architecture are somehow more authentic—more real and at once more fantastical and sur-*real*—appeals to Boontje. It allows for a freer approach, a speculation on the meaning of things, opening up and exploring sometimes light and witty, sometimes dark and brooding corners of the imagination and the surprises human expression affords us.

The nineteenth century contains the extremes Boontje admires. On the one hand it is the period of the gothic Dracula, Frankenstein, and tales from the Brothers Grimm and Hans Christian Andersen, all of which Boontje has devoured from childhood onwards, and John Everett Millais's richly decorative painting of the tragic *Ophelia* (1852), an image Boontje keeps on his studio wall. On the other hand the nineteenth century embodies the improving, decorous middle-class family life, technological advance and spectacular decorative schemes of the Arts and Crafts movement. These latter schemes and objects embody beauty and hand-making, rightness of material and richness of color and design alongside the concept of the good and simple life.

This affective unity of designing, making and living to emphasize the "therapeutic potential of the domestic interior" and the English view that "surroundings affect the individual's temperament and character"[8] quickly reverberated around Europe and beyond, reflecting, too, William Morris's socio-political edge. For example, as noted of Carl Larsson's famous late nineteenth-century home in the Swedish countryside, Lilla Hyttna: "The value of all objects in the Larsson home were connected to their beauty and utility, not their age or

188

a.

status;" the villa, as a "visual representation of progressive ideology elevated the house to a showplace of social idealism." [9] These are the attitudes and values Boontje upholds.

"The Arts and Crafts ideal of providing a sense of psycho-emotional well-being" can be related to today's ideas about "flow," the contented immersion in activity, and the sociopolitical happiness agenda, which roots well-being in locally shared experience rather than global commercial gain. [10] Murray Moss, Boontje's gallerist in New York, views Boontje as a latter-day William Morris, but with significant differences. [11] Like Morris, Boontje looks at history and acknowledges a wish for social engagement and the beauty of use based on a response to nature, but Boontje extends Morris's legacy by achieving globalized industrial production and embracing the latest technology. Boontje has given decoration a contemporary, mass-produced lease on life: what was for Morris a local arena, in terms of materials, production, and clients, has changed into a global one, where sourcing of materials, manufacturers, and orders for products is carried out in fifteen countries. Influenced also by his reading of Victor Papanek, Boontje consciously seeks a sustainable interconnectivity of production and consumption, exemplified by the tranSglass and Coopa Roca projects.

The craft and design movements Boontje admires are all underpinned by a progressive social and political dimension to design, but with different aesthetic and cultural outcomes. Ironically, the Bauhaus and De Stijl, which Boontje first studied closely, became the butt of the postmoderns, from the late sixties to the eighties, who included the Italian-based Superstudio, Archizoom, Memphis and Studio Alchimia, all influential in the development of Boontje's designs and philosophy. These were the countercultural theory-practitioners who confronted the conventions of the functionalists. Alessandro Mendini, founder of Studio Alchimia in 1976 and for whom Boontje worked in 1990, wrote: "The motivation for work lies not in its practical efficiency; the 'beauty' of an object consists of the love and magic with which it is designed, and in the soul which it contains." [12] Mendini wanted a creative milieu "where craftsmanship, industry, computer science, contemporary and non-contemporary techniques and materials can be mixed." [13] All these elements matter to Boontje on a daily basis.

Boontje was struck by the new manifestations of function and the freedom they engendered. It was an approach whose influence had reached Japan by the eighties and at that time the architect Arata Isozaki commented on Mendini's studio: "the products of their design encompass all the elements that compose the environment, such as technology, objects, surfaces, colors, materials, clothes, and furniture. They reduce each of these elements to its original state and then try to understand it from a new point of view."[14] Boontje was inspired not only by the Italians but by similar strategies proposed by, for example, the architect Bernard Tschumi, whom he had heard speak at Eindhoven.

Tschumi's presentation of his Parc de la Villette project for Paris with its de-structured spatial elements, tilted planes and red metal "follies," confronting the accepted notion of a park as green and natural space, inspired Boontje to see how form need not follow function in a rational procedure, where social hierarchies and uses of space and object were being literally and metaphorically dismantled.[15] Film and fiction were similarly engaged in jump-cut editing and labyrinths of oblique narrative, seeking to transcend the conventions of their medium. Among product designers, Ron Arad's concrete sound system and Daniel Weil's plastic bag radios also explored formal and functional inquiries, and Boontje drew on all such inspirations for his Garland light, Kvadrat textiles for the *Happy Ever After* installation and his **Wednesday**[p. 40–51] and **Doll**[p. 214–217] chairs. (Arad, generally skeptical about decorative objects for the home, nevertheless recognized the brilliance of Boontje's experiment with function in the Garland light: "as an exercise it was sort of really exciting to watch, you know, almost as exciting as the lemon squeezer. I think people see the lemon squeezer as an easy target to explain why Starck is not good. I think it explains how good he is and I think there's that also with the Garland light".)[16]

The Wednesday and Doll collections of chairs, like animated body-objects, and reflecting the fantasy world of dressing-up, indicated Boontje's connection to the work of fashion designers such as Martin Margiela, Yohji Yamamoto, Vivienne Westwood, and Hussein Chalayan, who were further disrupting conventions in imaginative ways. Fabrics were torn and seams exposed, underwear became outerwear and a garment's space for the neck could be an armhole.[17] The striking yet sometimes fragile form and materiality in relation to body and space is something Boontje engages with in his work. For example, his **Rough-and-Ready**[p. 25–31] furniture, inspired by the sight of raindrops falling on polythene sheeting in a London street, embodies the unexpected beauty of incidental, everyday materiality, while the Garland and Midsummer light, the Wednesday chairs and openwork textiles, for example, all review function from first principles, then load the space with textural exuberance.

In his exhibition installations, Boontje seeks a multilayered sensory experience, light, sound, touch, smell, partly inspired by the fashion shows of Alexander McQueen, with whom he has regularly worked and collaborated. Boontje learned from him the impact of display: As McQueen's *Untitled* Spring-Summer 1998 fashion show progressed, water from overhead sprinklers began to rain on the catwalk so that slowly, inexorably, the parading models became ever more expressively embodied in their soaking clothes, in defiance of their unique and handmade preciousness.

In altering ideas about how everyday things—buildings, clothes, furniture, and gadgets—function, semantic and experiential design trigger a new aesthetic. In London, the city in which Boontje's career flourished, design shifts accompanied social shifts since the sixties and seventies to a more widely publicized extent than in the Italy of Archizoom and Superstudio. Bourgeois values of stability and continuity were disrupted by youth culture and by "squatters," who occupied council houses lying empty for lack of public funds to renovate them. This tacitly accepted rupture allowed for a way of living to develop which relied on resourcefulness and ingenuity and on a critical stance to value in things. It carried over into strategies of design, which by the early eighties was based on "creative salvage," bricolage and the use of basic production equipment such as welding and glass-cutting tools. Ron Arad, Tom Dixon, Mark Brazier-Jones, Andre Dubreuil, and Danny Lane were exemplars of this design (r)evolution. The corporate design world of slick matt black furniture and consultancy for advertising and marketing clients was not their path. As Arad said, "I invented my own profession."[18]

These role models were coupled with the broader influence on Boontje of popular culture. In Europe and the States from the sixties onwards, an energetic engagement with mass communication, youth movements, radical politics and advertising brand imagery found cultural expression. This is reflected in Boontje's own enthusiasm for pop and punk music, fashion and art—languages of mass communication, which highlight the consumption of subversive glamour and desire. Elements of this street-wise connectedness yet anti-commercialism appeared in the London exhibitions *No Picnic* in 1998 and *Stealing Beauty* a year later, in both of which Boontje played a shaping and exhibiting role.[19]

In exploring what fellow exhibitor Anthony Dunne calls "a new direction for design," *Stealing Beauty*, in its analysis of materials, functions, forms and relationships, provided a loose "platform for all these different thoughts and experiments."[20] Louise Taylor, then exhibitions director at the Crafts Council said, "We knew we were onto something" and an enlarged, younger audience for design evolved: the architect David Adjaye, designer of *No Picnic*, was heard to say at the opening that he had never seen so many sneakers at the Crafts Council.[21] The crossover between craft, design, popular culture, and social comment was newly articulated in all the works in *No Picnic* and in *Stealing Beauty*, at the Institute of Contemporary Arts, but although the reputations of all the exhibitors, including Boontje's, began to grow from this time, the stance was individualistic and anti-commercial.

Clare Catterall, curator of *Stealing Beauty*, remembers Boontje's Rough-and-Ready furniture alongside other exhibitors' works: "What I found wonderful was there was a joy to it...the excitement and the buzz of living on the edge... Rough-and-Ready fitted perfectly because there were lots of elements in the exhibition that were quite dark...it did have this dark edge, looking at the underbelly, which I really liked." She picks up a Boontje resonance: "It was almost like a punk thing...this sense in punk of a great celebration of the dark and the heart; it was the same kind of thing, the strength of it and the empowerment."[22]

In opposition to commodifying luxury, Daniel Weil identifies Boontje's talent for the "banalization" of design, achieving extreme popularity for his work because, like Damien Hirst's art, it speaks directly to the emotions.[23] There is no self-conscious academicism, in common with his contemporary Joep van Lieshout—who founded Atelier van Lieshout in Rotterdam in 1994—whose work Boontje enjoys: "I like the message in the work, anarchic, self-sustainability." Like Hirst, who has made music videos, restaurants, and pop songs besides art, van Lieshout takes a non-hierarchical, almost promiscuous, approach to the production of ideas: "I don't care what people call it, as long as we can make what we want"[24]—and this includes furniture and interiors but also mobile homes, gadgets, weapons, equipment for slaughter houses, following psycho-analyst Wilhelm Reich's recommendation to acclaim "libidinous needs and seeing a comprehensive life-force in them."[25]

Boontje prizes the subjectivity of experience over objective judgment, appreciating the poetic minimal alteration of, for example, Martin Creed's 'value-free' crumpled ball of paper and Turner Prize-winning on-off light bulb and Gary Hume's paintings using household gloss paint and aluminum sheet, the imagery of females, plants and animals taken from photographs in magazines and art books, achieving "a conscious balancing act between cultural triviality, emotion and beauty."[26] Boontje's own work seeks similarly simple solutions: the **Cherry Pip** necklace [p. 120, 145], the **Cut Here** tattoo [p. 212–213], the self-generating imagery of **Inflorescence** [p. 112–117], the cut-down recycled bottles of **tranSglass** [p. 33–37]. In a banalized visual culture, what constitutes beauty, still a potent concern for Boontje and others, has shifted, as has the analysis of taste as an indicator of social distinction. Thus sociologist Pierre Bourdieu's work, which may have helped to analyze orthodox culture, "ignored the possiblilty of considering mundane things as a dynamic site of social change."[27]

In the context in which Boontje's career has burgeoned, the whole field of cultural analysis has progressively opened out. Yuniya Kawamura observes: "the avant-garde has become so popular that it has changed the definition of what is beautiful, which is often synonymous with what is fashionable...Globalization is about mobility across frontiers and also mobility of goods and commodities. It is also about the dissolution of the old structure and boundaries."[28] Adding to the findings of philosophers, literary theorists, and psychoanalysts, the anthropologists find their material culture investigations can produce "exotic" findings in local communities at home as much as in far-flung "other" locations; they find that subcultures and minority ethnic groups, sidelined by orthodox art and design historians, can provide fresh insights into public and private space and objects within them.

Boontje's background, life, and work exemplify this richness of hybrid experience, which he has distilled into a distinctive and independent approach to design. Material culture studies have found fruitful for recent study the artists and designers who have shaped the urban and domestic landscape through their interpretation of social, political, and cultural experience and through their changing conceptions of space and identity. "In the past the notion of home was associated with stability, dependability and identification, whereas homelessness meant change, instability, rootlessness and loss of identity. This opposition ceases to function in quite the same fashion in these times of comprehensively globalized circulation."[29]

These words of curator Boris Groys acknowledge that technological media, travel, and migration have changed our reception of products. This state is what is represented by Boontje's Rough-and-Ready furniture, embodying, as curator Boris Groys said in 2001, "the precarious balance between transience and permanence...everything seems extremely makeshift, bolted or glued together almost as if by accident. By the same token, these pieces of furniture also possess a certain humor and aesthetic appeal, and actually appear to be quite comfortable and homely, luring the viewer to stop and take a rest in the transitional state. Boontje's furniture has a Dadaistic and anarchic quality, but like [Kurt] Schwitters' *Merzbau*, they have a calming and relaxing effect as well."[30]

This "transitional state" in which contemporary artists and designers couch their work underlines their critical agendas. The wit of Boontje's work is always present as a strategy of giving pleasure, but also of showing critical awareness. The juxtaposition is evident in works he admires by Ilya and Emilia Kabakov, alongside whom he exhibited in the *Home/Homeless* show. In their installation, a cozy bourgeois interior is invaded by a radio voice, "exposed by modern media to an outside world relentlessly announcing its demands," while, paradoxically, also allowing "the world of modern tourism and accelerated mobility to be gently and cozily transferred for private display within one's own four walls."[31] This "media intrusion" is an indication of the contemporary complexity of the "real" world which interests Boontje and many of his contemporaries, who are aware of the responsibility designers can take for choosing to consider design as a sustainable and/or ethical, critical, and cultural activity.

The existential meets the everyday: new technology is allowing a mass market to customize and create design. The dictates of producers and the mantra of form follows function collapse when consumers are in charge of their personal computers, participants in the real/unreal world of information technology. The new producer-consumer partnership heralds new freedoms and new challenges. Boontje harnesses new technologies and materials to positive ends in his products, but also scans the futuristic horizon for context and ideas. The perhaps underlying utopianism of much of his outlook—a wish, as a designer, to make things better—is the result of confronting dystopian scenarios, via, for example, films by David Lynch, videos by Chris Cunningham, and readings of William Gibson, Neal Stephenson and Bruce Sterling, imagining the

Color selection for furniture.

effects of new psychic and technological space. The inspiration drawn from film and literary narratives is taken up amongst other contemporary designers such as Anthony Dunne, who names his approach *Design Noir*,[32] (echoing film noir), design as critique of the implications of our electronic, nano- and biotechnological universe and environmental unsustainability.

While Boontje's designs engage with all these aspects of the past and the future discussed so far, further features which contribute to his influential decorative language are his richness of color, insights into art history, uses of light and the telling of stories.

In his complex and striking use of color, Boontje corrals the personal influences of Holland and Sweden in his work, the former over-designed and over-populated with the hard primary colours of red, white, blue, black and yellow, the latter full of space and natural landscapes with soft colors. From Holland, too, Boontje draws on the rich tonal palette of Vermeer, Rembrandt, Hals, and the seventeenth-century still-life masters, and from Sweden images and narratives of indigenous folk art and vernacular objects. The colors in Boontje's work act as vital signifiers of emotional thought: the pure harmony of white, the brooding black and the use of Rococo pastels or a blood red which can appear joyous (**Table Stories**[p. 218–227], Midsummer lights) or transgressive (Wednesday table, cabinet and chairs, tattoos and the darker Kvadrat fabrics).

The colors, like his unerring eye for compositional graphic linearity and textural virtuosity, come from his close observation of the history of art, whether organic Gothic, or the Baroque, " a dynamic art" wherein "action and pathos, appealing to the observer's emotional participation, determine its character. The Baroque love of movement expresses itself in contrasts between concave and convex, dark and light," although drawn into a synthesis. This Baroque ideal produces "a new type of artist who was at once architect, painter, sculptor, and decorator," perhaps also a Boontje ideal, evident in his exhibitions, of creating the *Gesamtkunstwerk*, the total work of art.[33]

The Rococo period has been equally important for its evocation of "the light and joyful character of an earthly paradise," centered on eighteenth-century Parisian society "whose whole effort was directed towards the highest refinement of the pleasures of life."[34] Gardens, palaces, processions, spectacles, the ballet and opera were heightened arenas for creativity then, important also

Come Rain Come Shine design drawing.

as inspiration for Boontje's installations, but the dynamic in his work is always balanced by the delicate. Boontje's love of poetry in simplicity is grounded in the domestic interiors of paintings by artists such as van der Weyden, Vermeer, and Chardin, who "sought out the simplest subjects in the daily life of the street, the kitchen and the family circle. The world he cultivated was the tranquil, the inconspicuous, and the unheroic."[35]

This unassuming intimacy is perhaps most eloquently expressed by Boontje through his work with textile and paper. With these materials, Boontje imbues his designs with a soft definition of space, with movement, color and flexibility. Gilles Deleuze, writing philosophically on textile qualities, illuminates the appeal of Boontje's soft, flexible products. He describes "the fold that goes out to infinity as endlessly composing and recomposing, without inside or outside, beginning or end; a movement in which disparate elements encounter and separate, producing new modes of thought. Here, 'thinking' is not something we automatically do, or a knowledge we already have, but immanent, creative, experimental and critical,"[36] This is how Boontje encounters fabric or paper, feeling his way by cutting, draping, modeling, experimenting, not a pre-planned strategy but an evolution. There is, too, a voluptuousness in this process and the softness can be associated with fetish, with dreams, with flux—for Deleuze an association with the "fantastic curves of the Baroque, its swathing draperies and billowing clothes; the curling fruits and vegetables of its still-life paintings,"[37]—and with the luxuriantly deliquescent and symbolic Dutch still lifes.

For Boontje's design vocabulary is full of layering, hiding and revealing, enfolding, wrapping, compressing and extending (the lights, the card, the Tyvek curtains, the dressed chairs). His entangled forest of textile as displayed in, for example, his exhibition *Happy Ever After*, may evoke thoughts about Eva Hesse's extended wall pieces, such as *Untitled* (1969, latex over rope, wire, string): "questions of permanence, fragility, and materiality arise—as if these emotive, organic, at times 'formless' forms reflect back to us our own fragile and embodied subjectivity. For cloth, like the body, is a mediating surface through which we encounter the world."[38] These associations suggest how Boontje's decorative language should be understood, not stylistically but feelingly, a visual and physical embodiment of thought and experience.

As Modernism evolved, the architect Adolf Loos, in 1908, had decried ornament as a crime for its primitively "uncivilized" and "wasteful" aspects.[39] In the Modernist context, Boontje naturally favors the exemplar of Matisse, for whom decorative qualities offered a truer expression of the emotional range of people's thoughts and feelings, especially in his late paper cut collages such as *Mimosa*, (1949–51).[40] Matisse's legacy provided a conduit for the paradigm shift in the "feminization" of art and society in the postmodern era: "We are talking about the reemergence of certain neglected archetypal aspects of the human psyche, enabling more feminine ways of being to be reinstated in the general psychological patterns of society."[41] An assault on modern aesthetics which "has been colored, structured and controlled by a kind of compulsive masculinity... all that frenzy, ambition, competition and materialism," has been supplanted by " the importance of relationships and harmonious social interaction. This sense of deep affiliation, which breaks through the illusion of separateness and Cartesian dualism, is the highest principle of the feminine."[42] Boontje's work has flourished in this changed context and Hilary French, Head of the School of Architecture and Design at the RCA, notes his "feminized design aesthetic."[43]

In this regard, it is noteworthy how the debate on textile and specifically embroidery has developed since Roszika Parker's landmark socio-cultural analysis.[44] Where Boontje's textile material and techniques and qualities of softness, flexibility, and tactility might once have elicited ambivalence in those who viewed textile as a feminized, decorative category of design often linked with the transient world of fashion, today have been liberalized by fine art exhibitions which include embroidered works by, for example, Tracey Emin, Michael Raedecker, Ernesto Neto, Enrico David, and Grayson Perry.[45] "I know lots of other men who sew" Boontje says, and refers also to the masculine engagement with textiles and papercutting in folk traditions. "I always feel naturally at home in a female environment," Boontje adds, an experience grounded in his childhood. When Emily Campbell commissioned him to create a boudoir in collaboration with former *Elle Decoration* editor Ilse Crawford for the British Council exhibition *Hometime* in China, Boontje relished the opportunity, starting with Crawford's recommendation to him to read Virginia Woolf's *A Room of One's Own*: for Boontje, "stepping back in time to understand modern woman" made a lasting impression.

While femininity and decoration, airbrushed out of the masculine canon of Modernist industrial production, has been restored, another area of ambivalence within a Modernist avant-garde which privileged originality—that of referencing the old with the new, whether history, material or technology—has also been defused to Boontje's advantage, since his work is especially resonant precisely because of this combination. This is confirmed by the recollection of Alice Rawsthorn, former Director of the Design Museum, on first seeing tranSglass: "a brilliantly simple idea, beautifully executed and very poetic. It was impossible to look at each piece without wondering how the original wine bottle had been used in the past and what would happen to it in future. I also loved Tord's sense of balance between the old and the new. The new vessels were visibly made from old bottles, yet each intervention, such as the slicing of the glass, was crisp, clean, and dazzlingly contemporary."[46]

Boontje succeeds with new interpretations of old typologies: the chandelier, the "willow pattern" plate, the bench and swing seat, the lampshade, the upholstered chair, the chintz curtain. His work can be associated with the discourse in *Eternally Yours,* a late nineties book which made the case for a sustained, and sustainable, life for products: "Every new object should somehow respect old age. They should be bearers of 'old metaphors.'"[47] The frank association with folk art and vernacular design has been joyfully rehabilitated. A key image is the influential Droog designer Marcel Wanders' crochet chair, made of macramé carbon fiber cord soaked in plastic resin, then oven-fired within a metal frame and subsequently cut free. Wanders felt objects could be, "collections of mere information that everybody can interpret at will through their senses."[48]

The old is conjoined with the new. For Boontje, the use of new materials and methods are crucial to his designs, such as finding Tyvek for his Midsummer Light, achieving the 150 cm Garland light 'thread' through photo-etching on steel, or the printing on felt or computer-generated drawing of flowers on polyester for Kvadrat—an entirely new take on the traditions of embroidery, brocade, and damask—and the development of Inflorescence, a computerized, hands-off continuous wall decoration. Above all, however, a crucial 'material' for this industrial designer is light.

For Boontje, who has made the lighting object a cornerstone of his career, light is also an intangible material with which to create physical and emotional effects. He has observed this in key works which have inspired him: the late Shiro Kuramata's 1986 armchair for Vitra, entitled *How High the Moon,* made of nickel-plated shaped steel mesh, an ethereal form hovering in evanescent light and shadow; the incandescent beauty of Olafur Eliasson's *Weather Project* at Tate Modern in 2004, shifting the prone viewer between dream and reality; James Turrell's enclosed meditative light spaces, and Vermeer's paintings wherein "it is light alone which breathes life into his figures, conjuring ghosts of light rather than darkness; optical effect rather than the conceptual image."[49] In contrast Boontje is also inspired by the more troubling light and shadow of fire and flooding water of Bill Viola's videos and Caravaggio's religious paintings of "unprecedented extremity, intimacy, and actuality," the gospels painted as street life: "low and dirty realism... high-contrast lighting, chiaroscuro, a drama

Sketch for Babylon chair, 2004.

of violent glimpses and flashes coming out of pitch darkness."[50]

For Boontje, the illusions of light are foregrounded by shadow, just as his beloved European forests reveal and conceal in their dappled glades. The forest allusion gives an emotional, aesthetic and metaphorical charge to his products, "the impression of going deeper and deeper into a limitless world"[51] while the counterpoint of object and its shadow, critical to Western and Japanese aesthetics, suggests a ghostly otherness which writers on modernity have come to associate with the "hidden" presences in our everyday urban experience. So Boontje's work operates on two fronts, an interplay of the materiality and symbolism of nature with the materiality and symbolism of the city.

Walter Benjamin saw the "city as both dream world and catastrophe"[52] and for Boontje spectral ghosts of dark tales and darker corners of human experience haunt both the spaces and the objects of the everyday. Boontje speaks of Coppola's terrifying anti-Vietnam film *Apocalypse Now*, based on Conrad's *Heart of Darkness*, Tim Burton animations and gothic tales of the undead, secret societies, re-animated corpses, vampires and personal demons, a list which the authority Chris Baldick suggests evoke "a fear of historical reversion; that is, of the nagging possibility that the despotisms, buried by the modern age, may yet prove to be undead."[53] For Boontje, Mervyn Peake's *Gormenghast* trilogy is a favorite, "with its enormous scale, the dark, damp, rotting place, the grandeur and state of decay, I love the whole atmosphere." The entry of storytelling into contemporary design is enriching the design discourse.

In a compelling essay,[54] theorist Roger Luckhurst outlines the idea of lurking ghostly presences in the city street, evoked in contemporary literature and visual culture and embedded in the fabric of the city itself: "it is the Gothic revival of the late Victorian era that turns up repeatedly, clearly because this was the moment when a distinctively urban Gothic was realized...the movement of the genre from the wild margins of protestant Europe to the imperial metropolis of Victorian *fin de siecle*—precisely the trajectory that brings Count Dracula from the Carpathian mountains to the populous streets of London." Patrick Wright,[55] examining London today, haunts "places of inner-city ruin left by the vagaries of the market or hurriedly redesignated as 'heritage' sites." He perceived that "an interest in debris and human fallout is part of the New Baroque sensibility." Boontje, always sensible to the idea that modernity can't authentically erase the past, chose to identify Rough-and-Ready, his first personal work, literally with the detritus of the city. He did not deny the "ghosts of history" in the name of progress and the future as the early modernists did. It was an echo of those seventies squatters who appreciated living among the ruins.

Luckhurst produces a further kaleidoscope of writers to attest to the idea of modernity never actually escaping, or breaking with, the past and enumerating some here deepens our understanding of Boontje's trajectory. Anthony Vidler felt "the uncanny erupts in empty parking lots around abandoned or run-down shopping malls...in the wasted margins and surface appearances of post-industrial culture." In Christine Boyer's view, "we need to establish counter-memories...to resist and subvert the all-too-programmed and enveloping messages of our consumer culture." And Lynda Nead concluded that "the present remains permanently engaged in a phantasmatic dialogue with the past." Michel de Certeau's idea of an aesthetic of resistance to the modern, exemplified by Surrealists and Situationists who disrupted the totalized plan and notion of abstract city space would further support a view of Boontje's design approach and influences as being grounded in the idea of a spectral modernity. Jacques Derrida goes to the fundamentals: "it is necessary to introduce haunting into the very construction of a concept; of every concept, beginning with the concepts of being and time. This is what we would be calling here a hauntology."

A hauntology, the authentic locating of the past in the present in the city and the soul, allows for the rich narratives Boontje seeks in his work. The ghostly, the spectral, is also evident in contemporary fashion design Boontje admires, which theorist Caroline Evans equates with a Freudian return of the repressed, because fashion, intent on being new, in fact in the process is always recovering the past. The clothes of McQueen, Westwood and John Galliano especially underline this in their engagement with historical reference and storytelling.[56]

In 1997, Ed van Hinte wrote, "it is the responsibility of designers to communicate to people, to tell them stories by the objects they create"[57] Clare Catterall saw this inclination in Boontje: "I love the way that he was continually searching... after the birth of Evie he decided he wanted life to be more like a fairy wonderland for her sake, and he suddenly recognized the importance of innocence."[58] In *The Lure of the Object*, Marcia Pointon states that objecthood in modernity, found in Surrealism, Dada, and Minimalism, is closely intertwined with "psychoanalysis, with its strong proposal of objects as everywhere worked by the vicissitudes of desire, its modalities of attachment and detachment, insistence and loss."[59]

These are the archetypal themes of fairy tales and myths, which for Boontje are a fundamental inspiration in his work, especially when told and retold by Hans Christian Andersen and the Brothers Grimm. Boontje is not a modern or postmodern, but a transmodern designer, for whom fiction infiltrates and reworks the conventional dialectics between design theory and practice and ignores design history's sequence of stylistic movements. Layers of reality and the imagination are fused. As Marina Warner writes: "Fairy tales often engage with issues of light and darkness...they have attempted to challenge received ideas and raise questions,"[60] while in illuminating the fruits of struggle and hope, sometimes encoding subversion and protest, fairy tales "unite societies across barriers of all kinds."[61]

Russell Hoban's introduction to Grimms' tales says that the making of fiction involves asking 'What if?' and that, in undertaking this, they "worked not for some prettified ideal of childhood, but for the ongoing 'What if?' that is mankind."[62] Scientists tell us that "the person who is prevented from dreaming cannot function properly when awake,"[63] and as the many metaphors of Shakespeare attest, which involve knowing ourselves better through experiencing dream-like contexts, ghosts, double identities, tricks of nature and the fates—renewal and enlightenment found when winter turns to spring or the tempest subsides. Like the near contemporaneous Baroque artists seeking to "blur the boundary between appearance and reality...the goal that was sought was a heightened sense of reality in which the natural and the miraculous fuse into a great whole."[64] Boontje as storyteller echoes this discourse on the real and the imagined, on nature and artifice, on the temporal life and idealized desires, enriching our quotidian lives whilst alerting us to its fragility. Perhaps Boontje's vases for Moroso best symbolize this, with their two-faced floral symbolism—love and ideal beauty on one side but on the reverse death and decay, when "flowers wither like old and overly made-up dowagers."[65]

All Boontje's work is layered, physically and metaphorically. Philip Dodd, former Director of the ICA, who commissioned the *Stealing Beauty* exhibition in 1999, wrote then: "Design is often a problem for over-tidy minds. It looks so many ways at once: towards the industrial and the artisan, towards culture and commerce, towards art and product, towards aesthetics and ethics."[66] Boontje does all these things. Alice Rawsthorn is wary of talking about an avant garde," a problematic term in design right now, as it is in many other areas of visual culture, where experimentation is co-opted so speedily into the mainstream."[67] Boontje himself eschews the imperatives of constant change and progress in favor of the humanistic side of design and its enduring sociopolitical, communicative role. Since he is not interested in stylistic cycles but in what he calls "the big issues"—identity, memory, history, love, loss, redemption—he appreciates their powerful expression in some of Damien Hirst's work, especially *Mother and Child Divided,* and in the work of German artists such as Anselm Kiefer, Joseph Beuys, Gerhard Richter and Hans Haacke.

At the Venice Biennale in 1993, Haacke created his installation entitled *Germania* by smashing up the marble floor of the German pavilion. Recalling his experience of seeing this, Boontje says, "It had a huge impact on different levels." Viewing Haacke's metaphor for a post-reunification Germany based on ruptured foundations, Boontje was moved by the direct physical impact: "You could hear people on the smashed floor, the shock, the act of violence in that. You don't add, you only destruct; don't live life to express status, live life in a different way." The conviction of these thoughts carries into Boontje's work such as tranSglass: "don't add, only take something away,"he says.

Haacke's artistic practice has also encompassed curatorial interventions in museums and questions the authority, and authorship, of curators who "frame and (unwittingly) are framed."[68] It is in these institutions that reputations are historically enshrined. For a designer upholding egalitarian living and freedom of expression, the inherent elitism of the life of products in museums is ambivalent territory for Boontje, whose work is now represented in major collections of the world. He questions the role of museum displays which convey typologies of function rather than possibilities of meaning or which automatically parade the classical canon: "All design collections have Arne Jacobsen. That's fine, but it doesn't mean you have an incomplete or worse museum if you don't have an Arne Jacobsen chair and you have something else." Boontje views his work as "a vehicle to translate into something thoughts about the way the world is and what it should be." So in a museum culture, continues Boontje, "the questions you ask are cultural questions. Which part of a culture is being defined by the object? Take, say, a collection of 1960s Pop dresses. If you would wear and walk round at that time in that world, how would you feel? What does that say about you? What is your position in the world at that moment? These are the interesting things to wonder. Definitely not about how it is made."

What, then, does Boontje seek to define with his work? His answer is conclusive: "A very positive, forward-looking, caring, loving world."

Endnotes

1. In conversation with Martina Margetts, author, 30 June, 2006.

2. Interview with author, 12 June 2006.

3. All quoted speech by Tord Boontje is from conversations with the author, March–July 2006.

4. See Erwin Panofsky, *Renaissance and Renascences in Western Art*. Paladin, 1970, p. 160 and p.165.

5. Martin Heidegger, "Building, Dwelling, Thinking" in *Poetry, Language, Thought*. London: Harper Collins 2001, p. 149–56; Gaston Bachelard, The Poetics of Space. Boston: Beacon Press, 1994, chapters 1,2,4; Sigmund Freud, "The Uncanny" in Werner Hamacher and David Wellbery (eds.) *Writings on Art and Literature*. Palo Alto: Stanford University Press, 1997, p.193–233.

6. Sigmund Freud, ibid. p. 200.

7. Christopher Reed (ed.) *Not At Home: The Suppression of Domesticity in Modern Art and Architecture*. London: Thames and Hudson, 1996, both p.163.

8. ibid., p. 82.

9. ibid., both p. 90.

10. ibid., p. 86 and contemporary writings eg. Mihaly Czikszentmihaly, *Flow: The Classic Work on How to Achieve Happiness*, London 2002 and Richard Layard *Happiness: Lessons From a New Science*. New York: Allen Lane, 2005.

11. View expressed by Murray Moss in interview with the author, New York, 18 April, 2006.

12. Alessandro Mendini, "The Alchimia Manifesto", July 1985, in Kazuko Sato, *Alchimia: Contemporary Italian Design*. Berlin: TACO Verlagsgesellschaft und Argentur mbH, 1988, p.6.

13. ibid, p.6.

14. Foreword by Isozaki in Andrea Branzi, *The Hot House: Italian New Wave Design*, London: Thames and Hudson, 1984, p.6.

15. Bernard Tschumi, *Event-Cities 2*. Boston: MIT Press, 2000, whole project documented p. 44–225.

16. Interview with the author, April 2006.

17. Yuniya Kawamura, *Fashion-ology: An Introduction to Fashion Studies*, London: Berg, 2005, p.105.

18. op. cit. (See also Arad's comments in special issue on London, Icon, issue 028, October 2005, p. 101).

19. *No Picnic*, Crafts Council, London 9 July–30 August, 1998; *Stealing Beauty*, Institute of Contemporary Arts, London 3 April–23 May 1999.

20. Interview with the author, 3 July, 2006.

21. Interview with the author, 6 July, 2006.

22. From interviews with the author, April 2006.

23. Interview with the author, April 2006.

24. Quoted in Burkhard Reimschneider and Uta Prosenick, *Art for the Millennium*, Cologne: Taschen, 2000, p. 314. (See also van Lieshout profile in *Icon*, issue 029, November 2005, London, p. 92–98.)

25. ibid., Reich quoted in Yilmaz Dziewior's commentary on van Lieshout, p. 314.

26. ibid., p. 215.

27. Judy Attfield commenting on Bourdieu in her book *Wild Things: The Material Culture of Everyday Life*. Oxford: Berg, 2000, p. 93.

28. op. cit.

29. Boris Groys, Vision Art Exhibitions catalogue: *Home/Homeless*, BoO1 City of Tomorrow, European Housing Expo, Malmo, Sweden, 17 May–16 September 2001, p. 26.

30. ibid., p. 39.

31. ibid., p. 40.

32. Anthony Dunne and Fiona Raby, *Design Noir: The Secret Life of Electronic Objects*. London: August Birkhauser, 2001.

33. Ursual Hatje (ed.) *The Styles of European Art*, London: Thames and Hudson, 1965, p. 333.

34. ibid., p. 334.

35. ibid., p. 381.

36. Letter from the Editors, Penina Barnett on behalf of Janis Jefferies and Doran Ross, *Textile: The Journal of Cloth and Culture*, Vol 1, Issue 1, March, London, 2003.

37 and 38. ibid., p. 3.

39. Adolf Loos, "Ornament and Crime" (1908) reprinted in Yehuda Safran and Wilfried Wang (eds.) *The Architecture of Adolf Loos*. London: Arts Council of Great Britain, 1985, p. 100–104.

40. See James Trilling, *The Language of Ornament*, London: Thames and Hudson, 2001, p. 211–212.

41. Suzie Gablik, *The Re-enchantment of Art*. London: Thames and Hudson, 1991, p. 124.

42. ibid., p. 127,128.

43. Interview with the author, April 2006.

44. Roszika Parker, *The Subversive Stitch: Embroidery and the Making of the Feminine*. London: The Women's Press, 1984.

45. For example *Loose Threads*, Serpentine Gallery, London, 2001; Grayson Perry, Guerilla Tactics, Stedelijk Museum, Amsterdam, 2002; *Boys Who Sew*, Crafts Council Gallery, London, 2005.

46. Email exchange with author, 4 May–7 June, 2006.

47. Ed van Hinte (ed.) *Eternally Yours: Visions on Product Endurance*. Rotterdam: 010 Publishers, 1998.

48. ibid.

49. John Jacob, *The Complete Paintings of Vermeer*. New York, Penguin, 1987.

50. Tom Lubbock, *The Independent*, London, 29 July 2006.

51. Gaston Bachelard, op. cit., p. 185.

52. Quoted in Emma Dexter's essay "London 1990–2001" in Iwona Blazwick (ed.), *Century City: Art and Culture in the Modern Metropolis*. London: Tate Publishing, 2001, p. 79.

53. Chris Baldick, *The Oxford Book of Gothic Tales*. Oxford: Oxford University Press, 1992.

54. Roger Luckhurst, "The Contemporary London Gothic and the Limits of the Spectral Turn," *Textual Practice* 16 (3), 2002, p. 527–546.

55. The references in this and the next paragraph are fully documented in Luckhurst.

56. Caroline Evans, *Fashion at the Edge*. New Haven: Yale University Press, 2003, p. 51.

57 and 58. op. cit.

59. Marcia Pointon in Stephen Melville (ed.), *The Lure of the Object*. Williamstown, MA: Sterling and Francine Clark Art Institute, 2005, p. viii.

60. Marina Warner, *From the Beast to the Blonde: on Fairy Tales and Other Tellers*. New York: Chatto and Windus, 1994, p. 410.

61. Warner quoting from Italo Calvino, *Six Memos for the Next Millennium*. New York: Vintage Classics, 1996.

62. Russel Hoban, introduction to Grimms' *Household Tales*. London: Pan Macmillan, 1977, p. 12.

63. ibid.

64. Ursula Hatje (ed.) op. cit., p. 333.

65. Georges Bataille "The Language of Flowers" in *Visions of Excess*. Minneapolis: University of Minnesota Press, 1985, p. 12.

66. Catalogue, p6, to *Stealing Beauty* exhibition, op. cit.

67. op. cit.

68. Hans Haacke, catalogue to his *Give & Take* exhibition, Serpentine Gallery and Victoria and Albert Museum, London 30 January–1 April 2001.

201 (previous page) and 203. **Wilderness**, Kvadrat (2005)   202. **Sleeping Rose**, Kvadrat (2005)

204. **Eternal Summer**, Kvadrat (2005)   205. **Wilderness**, Kvadrat (2005)

208. **Pressed Flowers,** Kvadrat (2005)   210–211 (overleaf). **Prima Vera Tiles,** Bardelli (2005)

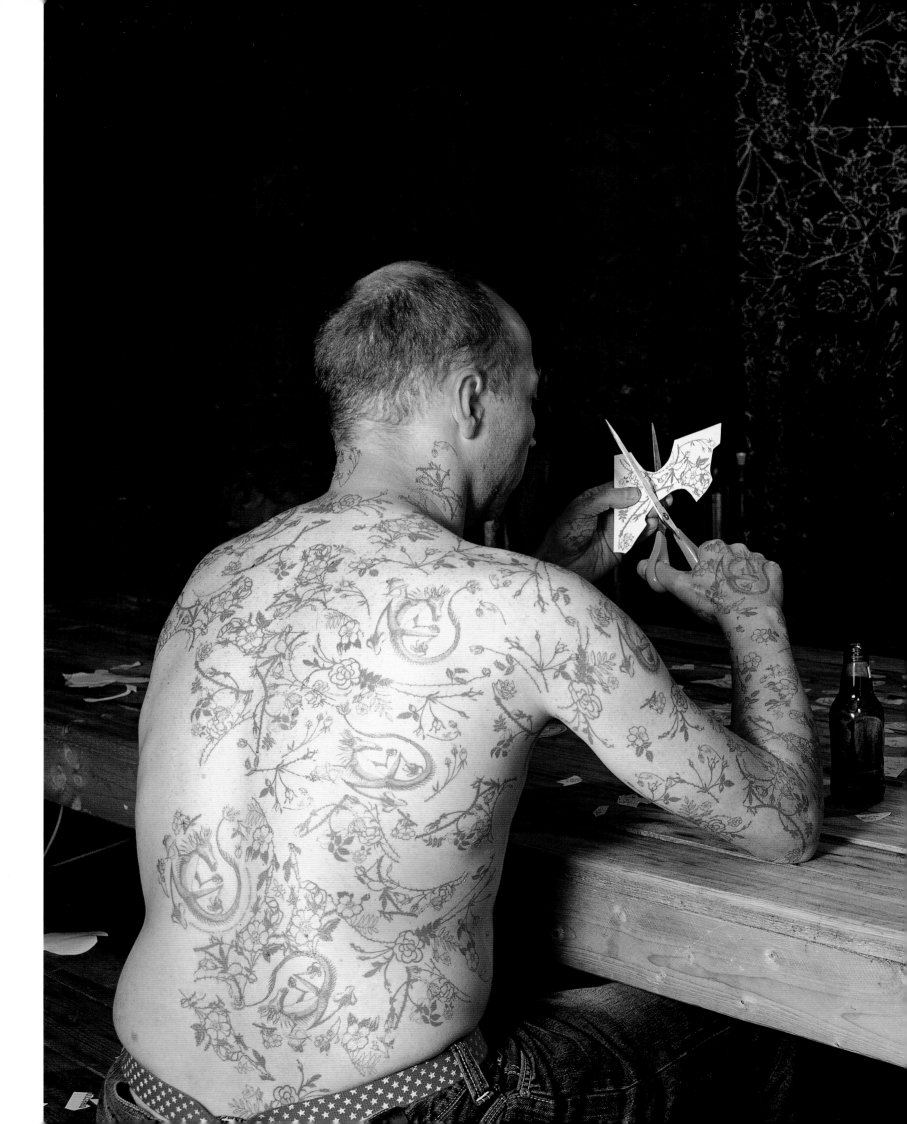

212–213. **Cut Here** tattoo, Chi Ha Pura (2005)

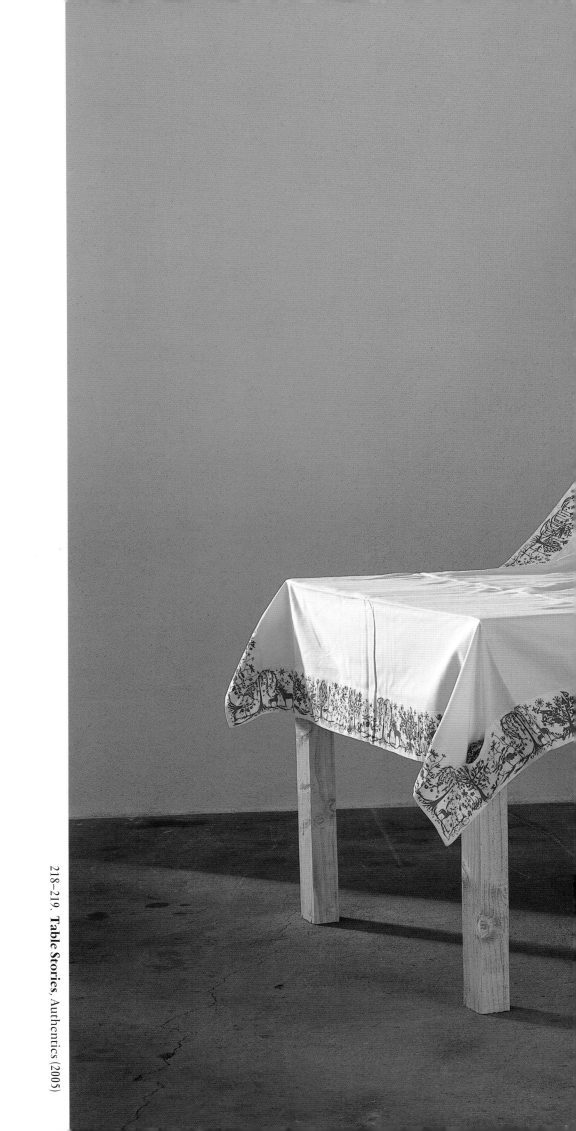

228–229 (previous pages) and 230, 231. **Christmas 2006**, Target (2006)

228–229. **Winter Wonderland**, Swarovski Crystal Gallery, Innsbruck (2006)

232–233. **Winter Wonderland**, Swarovski Crystal Gallery, Innsbruck (2006)

244-245. **The Other Side**, Moroso (2006)

Chronology

1968

Born in Enschede, Netherlands.

1986

Enrolls at the Design Academy in Eindhoven to study industrial design.

1989

Work placement in New York.

1990

Works for the Studio Alchimia design group in Milan.

1991

Graduates from the Design Academy, Eindhoven.

1992

Moves to London to study for a master's degree in industrial design at the Royal College of Art; meets artist Emma Woffenden who has been his partner ever since.

1994

Graduates from the Royal College of Art.

1995

Designs exhibitions with Ulf Moritz in Amsterdam.

1996

Moves to Peckham, south London, where he sets up a studio with Emma.

1997

Collaborates with Emma to produce the tranSglass collection of glass vases, beakers and carafes made from used beer and wine bottles.

1998

Makes the Rough-and-Ready Chair in kit form from strips of pre-cut wood using blankets as upholstery; starts to design products, such as eyewear, for the fashion designer Alexander McQueen.

1999

Participates in the *Stealing Beauty: British Design Now* exhibition at the Institute of Contemporary Arts, London.

2000

Tord and Emma's daughter Evelyn is born; exhibits his Rough-and-Ready furniture at Tate Modern, London.

2001

Designs the Wednesday Light and manufactures it on a batch production basis; develops a collection of vases for Dartington Crystal.

2002

Returns to the Royal College of Art to teach industrial design; designs two chandeliers—Blossom and Horse—for Swarovski's *Crystal Palace*; develops Garland, a less expensive version of the Wednesday Light for Habitat; solo exhibition at the Barrett Marsden Gallery, London.

2003

Participates in the Great Brits exhibition organized by the Design Museum and British Council at the 2003 Milan Furniture Fair; launches the Inflorescence project in collaboration with Andrew Shoben and Andrew Allenson; shortlisted for the Design Museum's *Designer of the Year* award.

2004

Works with Moroso on the *Happy Ever After* exhibition in Milan. Starts to design the collection of textiles for Kvadrat and outgrows the studio in Peckham.

2005

Table Stories for Authentics is launched, shows *Carousel* in Milan and moves to France. In the midst of the chaos of the new studio, Target commissions the largest project to date. Intense design work and cross-Atlantic travel start.

2006

After a very cold but beautiful winter, the studio is still in chaos. *Winter Wonderland* opens in Innsbruck. Builds a tree house in the garden and organizes the studio. The Target project gets launched on the 1st of November. Makes an interactive installation and Christmas tree in Union Square, New York.

Installations

Wednesday—Prague

The British Council Window Gallery
Prague
9 January–23 March 2001

Tord Boontje's first solo show, curated by Andreé Cooke
with new work commissioned by the British Council.
This exhibition took place in the windows of the British
Council's offices in a main shopping street. Here
Boontje showed for the first time the start of the
Wednesday Collection including the first batch of twelve
Wednesday Lights. The exhibition was a result of one
year of research in historical decorative techniques and
the start of Boontje's new design approach.

During the first night of installing the work, Boontje
cut his hand on one of the Wednesday Lights and had
to be stitched up in the hospital. This caused the
Wednesday Light to be packaged in a box as it was
regarded as too unsafe, later this was remedied by the
Garland version of the light.

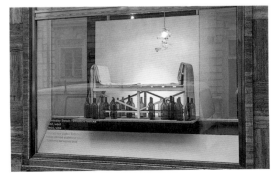

Wednesday—London

Applied Arts Agency
London WC1
10 May–17 May 2001

A derelict butcher's shop formed the backdrop of the
first installation of the Wednesday collection in London,
hosted by Applied Arts Agency.

251

Silent Light

with Alexander McQueen
Victoria and Albert Museum
London
December 2004

In collaboration with Alexander McQueen, Boontje
designed a petrified and frozen pine tree. The tree is
mounted on a turntable and slowly spins around,
reflecting in a mirrored setting. The tree was made using
over 100,000 crystals that were assembled by hand
around a 6-meter tall metal skeleton. The Silent Light
tree was later transferred to the Swarovski Crystal
World in Wattens, Austria.

The Other Flower Show

Victoria and Albert Museum
London
29 May–11 July 2004

Set at a date to coincide with the annual Chelsea
Flower Show, the V&A invited ten artists to transform
a standard garden shed. Boontje raised his shed onto
a metal structure, creating a covered outside space and
a closed upstairs room. The shed was spray stenciled
using the Until Dawn curtains. The downstairs room
had a hammock surrounded by cut-out tyvek curtains.
Inside a video played a slow motion walk through
Greenwich park. The Sweetie Cushion was the first
prototype made by Moroso.

253

Boudoir

with Ilse Crawford
Exhibit at *Hometime*
Guangzhou, Beijing, Shanghai and Chongquing, China
19 September 2003–28 January 2004

The British Council commissioned Ilse Crawford and
Tord Boontje to design a boudoir as part of a traveling
group exhibition where a selection of artists were asked
to design a room for an imagined house. *Boudoir* was
conceived as a private room for a modern woman.
The room became an assembly of different people's
work. The walls are made up of a wardrobe of clothes,
some secondhand, some made by Rebecca Early.
A large fiberglass dish, 'The Temple', by Jephson Hill
Robb functioned as a cross between a bed and a sofa,
The floor incorporated interactive sound by Andrew
Shoben and five paintings by Michael Grant were placed
around the room.

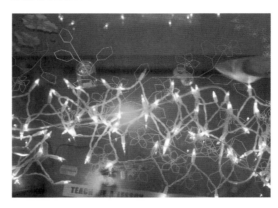

Happy Ever After

Showroom Moroso
Via Pontaccio 8/10, Milan
15–19 April 2004

Forever

Aram Store
110, Drury Lane, London
23 September – 2 October 2004

The End

Moss Gallery
Greene Street, New York
January 2005

Invitations for the three exhibitions that signaled the
collaboration between Moroso and Tord Boontje.

Happy Ever After

Showroom Moroso
Via Pontaccio 8/10, Milan
15–19 April 2004

An installation that was the first collaboration with
Moroso. The space was filled with experiments and
thoughts about textiles, furniture, early prototypes
and one-off pieces from the Wednesday Collection.

256

257

The End

Moss Gallery
Greene Street, New York
January 2005

Continuing the work with Moroso, many pieces that were shown at *Happy Ever After* in Milan had now been developed to production pieces. In addition to the Moroso pieces, *The End* also included Come Rain Come Shine chandelier, Blossom Chandelier, Shadow Fabric prototype, Paper Vases (later these became Thinking of You vases) and jewelry made from cherry pips.

Shadowplay

Terminal One, Heathrow Airport
London
Commissioned by British Airways
2005

Built into a wall in the business class and first class
lounge is a large screen; shadows and lights appear
in a changing, random pattern. "This collage of imagery
works as a kind of window in the space, creating a
meditative view for travelers" (TB).

Kean Street

Facade
Kean Street, Covent Garden, London
2003

Commissioned as a public artwork by the developer of a new residential and office building in Covent Garden, the large copper garland gives some nature back to a tree-less street. The copper material is untreated and will patinate over time.

Fashion Rocks

Grimaldi Forum, Monte Carlo
2006

For a one-night rock concert and charity dinner,
Swarovski and the Princes Trust had commissioned
the design of the dining room for a thousand people.
The installation featured the first Ice Branch chandeliers,
of which fifty were hung in the space. The table
centerpiece, Ice Vase was made with long necklaces
of crystals, most of which walked away with the
diners that evening.

CFDA Fashion Awards

New York Library, New York
2006

The CFDA and Swarovski commissioned the setting of the entrance hall for the yearly award ceremony. The space functioned as a cocktail area and background for television interviews. Live foliage and enlarged artificial blooms were combined around the space. The flowers were made from aluminum, encrusted with graduated colors of crystal.

Carousel

Alexander McQueen store
Via Verdi, Milan
2005

As a showcase during the Milan Furniture Fair, the clothes of McQueen and the products of Boontje were mixed in the store. The installation featured the Moroso Doll Chairs for which McQueen had designed special covers that can be worn as dresses (p. 214–217). Clothes from the Spring/Summer collection were fitted onto the chairs as well, as shown on this page.

The Forest of KARAKUSA:
Tord Boontje and the Arabesque

House of Shiseido
Ginza, Tokyo
7 February – 19 March 2006

Shisheido had recognized links between their use of the arabesque ornament in graphics, advertising and packaging and the work of Boontje. The Japanese tradition of the arabesque (Karakusa—meaning China Grass) follows roots to classic Chinese two-dimensional patterns. The arabesque that Boontje uses in his work, often has a three dimensional form.

For this installation several new pieces were developed in the studio, including the Petit Jardin metal bench, one-off fabrics, a black wood bench and a glass swing, Dreaming/Floating. The second part of the exhibition, upstairs, showed an extensive archive of Boontje's products.

Catalogue of designs

2003

Shadow Light	metal, printed acetate	Studio Tord Boontje
Rocking Chair	wood, blanket, cotton	Studio Tord Boontje
Black Bird Chair	wood, textile, embroidery	Studio Tord Boontje
Patched Chair	wood, textile, embroidery	Studio Tord Boontje
Pierced Chair	wood, textile, punching, in two colors	Studio Tord Boontje
Inflorescence vases	nesting vases	Studio Tord Boontje
Wednesday Glass	glass tableware; five shapes	Dartington Crystal
Abu Dhabi	lighting proposal	Abu Dhabi Works Deptartment
Night Blossom	chandelier; crystal	Swarovski
Wall Flowers	chandelier	Swarovski
Fairy Tail	greeting card; paper	Artecnica

2004

Midsummer Light	light; die-cut tyvek	Artecnica
Until Dawn	curtain; die-cut tyvek	Artecnica
Come Rain Come Shine	chandelier in three colorways, s/m/l	Artecnica/Coopa Roca
Witch Chair	metal, foam, leather	Moroso
Princess Chair	antique chair, silk, embroidery	Moroso
Forrest Chair	metal, foam, textile	Moroso
Paradise Chair	metal, foam, textile	Moroso
Red Veil Chair	metal, foam, textile	Moroso
Pirate Chair	metal, foam, textile	Moroso
Sweetie	seat; foam, cotton	Moroso
Dondola	swing seat; metal, foam, wool	Moroso
Revolution Arm Chair	seat; metal, foam, wool	Moroso
Ting Ting Ting	chandelier; crystal	Swarovski

2005

Bunny Chair II	wood, textile, embroidery	Studio Tord Boontje
Horse Chair II	wood, textile, embroidery	Studio Tord Boontje
Oval Table	steel, printed corian or glass top	Moroso
Doll Chair	metal, foam, textile	Moroso
Dress Chair	cover with Alexander McQueen	Moroso
Happy Rocker	rocking chair; steel, wood, wool	Moroso
Sweetie	seat; foam, cotton	Moroso
Little Flowers Falling	curtain/screen; microfiber, laser cut	Moroso
Fallen Flowers	curtain/screen; microfiber, laser cut	Moroso
Closer	sofa; wood, foam, textile, in two sizes	Moroso
Magic	upholstery textile; wool/nylon	Kvadrat
Princess	upholstery textile; wool/nylon, screen print	Kvadrat
Prince	upholstery textile; wool/nylon, screen print	Kvadrat
Happy	upholstery textile; wool/nylon, screen print	Kvadrat
Heaven Scent	upholstery textile; wool/nylon, screen print	Kvadrat
Dreamer	curtain textile; treviera cs	Kvadrat
Sleeping Rose	curtain textile; treviera cs, screen print	Kvadrat
Wilderness	curtain textile; treviera cs, digital printing	Kvadrat
Shadow	curtain textile; treviera cs, digital printing	Kvadrat
Nectar	curtain textile; burn-out, screen print	Kvadrat
Pressed Flowers	curtain textile; burn-out	Kvadrat
Eternal Summer	curtain textile; treviera, laser cut fabric	Kvadrat
Prima Vera	tiles; ceramic, two colorways	Bardelli
Thinking Of You – Here	vase, etched metal	Artecnica
Thinking Of You – Now	vase, etched metal	Artecnica
Thinking Of You – Forever	vase, etched metal	Artecnica
Icarus	light; extruded polyester	Artecnica
Flora	garland; copper	Artecnica
Puddles	mirrors; polished stainless steel	Artecnica
Cut Here	stick-on tattoo, paper	Chi Ha Pura
Table Stories	plates; porcelain, four sizes in three colorways	Authentics
Table Stories	bowls; porcelain, four sizes in three colorways	Authentics
Table Stories	cups; porcelain, four sizes in three colorways	Authentics
Table Stories	tablecloth; cotton in three colorways	Authentics
Table Stories	place mat; cotton in three colorways	Authentics
Table Stories	glasses; cotton in three colorways	Authentics
Table Stories	candle holder; glass, in two sizes	Authentics
Spring Blossom	chandelier, crystal	Swarovski
Autumn Blossom	chandelier, crystal	Swarovski
Ice Branch	chandelier, crystal	Swarovski

2006

Petit Jardin	bench; metal, laser cut	Studio Tord Boontje
Dreaming/Floating	swing; glass, string	Studio Tord Boontje
Black Bench	bench; wood, nails	Studio Tord Boontje
Bon Bon	coffee table, printed corian	Moroso
Nest	garden chair; rotation molded plastic	Moroso
Hello Lovely	mirror; printed glass, three sizes	Moroso
The Other Side	vases and bowls; ceramic	Moroso
Dragon Tray	tray; silver	De Vecchi
Rialto Deco	coffee table; glass	Fiam
Table Stories	espresso cups; porcelain, in three colorways	Authentics
Table Stories	cups and saucers; porcelain, in three colorways	Authentics
Table Stories	salad bowl; porcelain, two sizes in three colorways	Authentics
Table Stories	coffee mugs; porcelain, in three colorways	Authentics
Little Field of Flowers	rug; die-cut wool	Nanimarquina
Christmas '06	product collection; thirty-five Christmas products	Target

Solo exhibitions and installations

2003

Silent Light, Christmas tree, Victoria & Albert Museum.
Wild Silk, installation, Design Museum, London; Hermes.
Summer, installation; Habitat café, London.
Boudoir with Ilse Crawford, traveling exhibition,
five cities, China; British Council.

2004

Kean Street, building façade; copper; Jonathan Stein.
Pearl Candelabra, restaurant table lighting; Delano.
Hotel, Miami.
Happy Ever After, installation, Milan; Moroso.
Forever, installation, London; Aram/Moroso.

2005

The End, installation; Moss Gallery, New York.
Fashion Rocks, event installation; Swarovski.
Shadow Play, installation; metal, plastic, fiber optic;
British Airways.

2006

*The Forest of KARAKUSA: Tord Boontje and the
Arabesque*, House of Shiseido, Tokyo.
CFDA, event installation, New York, Swarovski/CFDA
Winter Wonderland, permanent installation, Innsbruck;
Swarovski.
Target–Christmas '06, stores; Christmas store
decorations; communication; art direction for
advertising; Target.
Union Square, public interactive projection; Target.

Selected group shows

1997

100% Design, London.

1998

Powerhouse:UK, London.
No Picnic, Crafts Council, London.
100% Design, London.

1999

Designers Block, London.
Lost and Found: Critical Voices in New British Design,
British Council; 1999–2000.
Stealing Beauty: British Design Now, Institute for
Contemporary Arts, London; 3 April–23 May.

2000

Salviati meets London, London;
30 September–30 October.

2001

Industry of One, Crafts Council, London;
1 February–25 March.
Dead, The Roundhouse, London; 2–10 March.
Century City: Art and Culture in the Modern Metropolis,
Tate Modern, London; 1 February–29 April.
Wednesday, The British Council Window Gallery,
Prague; 9 January–23 March.
Home/Homeless, Malmö; 17 May–16 September
Wednesday, Applied Arts Agency, London;
10 May–17 May.
Global Tools: Spin off, KlausEngelhorn22, Vienna;
12 July–31 August.
Global Tools, Kunstlerhaus, Vienna;
11 July–9 September.
The Unexpected, Sotheby's, New York;
14 October–22 October.

2002

Crystal Palace, off-site venue, Milan; 10–15 April.
Crystal Palace, Borough Market, London;
26 September–29 September.
Wednesday, Barrett Marsden Gallery, London;
6 September–12 October.
Pattern Crazy, Crafts Council, London;
4 July–1 September.
Crystal Palace, Design Museum, London;
27 September 2002–5 January 2003.

2003

Great Brits, Design Museum and British Council, Milan;
9–14 April.
Designer of the Year, Design Museum, London;
1 February–27 June.
Hometime, 19 September 2003–28 January 2004.
Tian He Stadium, Guangzhou;
19–28 September 2003.
China Millennium Monument, Beijing;
23 October–11 November 2003.
Shanghai Super Brand Mall, Shanghai;
28 November–21 December 2003.
Chongqing Gymnasium, Chongqing;
5–28 January 2004.

2004

The Other Flower Show, Victoria & Albert Museum,
London; 29 May–11 July 2004

2005

Miami Art Basel, Moss Gallery, Miami.

Acknowledgments

Tord Boontje

I would like to thank many people who have made this book possible. It has been wonderful to work so extensively with my two favorite photographers, Angela Moore and Annabel Elston. They broke all records for getting covered in mud, soot, smoke, paint and flowers, working at the crack of dawn and the middle of the night. Paul Neale, whose work at Graphic Thought Facility, I have admired for a long time. His passion for the art of making books, extensive knowledge of production processes and creative freedom has definitely shaped this book as something special.

Martina Margetts is not only a lovely person but also one of the most incisive and clever people that I have had the pleasure of knowing. Since my time as a student at the Royal College of Art, and in many conversations since then, she has always managed to show me references to my work and insights that were new to me (as well as teaching me a new word or two).

From Rizzoli, thank you to Charles Miers whose passion for fairy tales and uncompromising attitude to publishing have led to the commissioning of this book. (sorry for going so over the budget, it was worth it). Ian Luna, who has been the easiest editor and supporter of the whole project, has managed to produce what could have been a long term project; thanks.

Besides the book, the content could not have been there if it had not been for all the friends, teachers, colleagues and commissioners who have supported me through all these years. My mother, brother and sister have always been there for me and encouraged what I did. This encouragement has been fundamental to what I have been able to do.

A big thank you to the team in the studio and all the people who have worked in the studio in the past—either in crowded small spaces or big and too cold, always too few or too many instructions and never enough time. You all made it happen.

Most of all I wish to thank Emma for all her support, wisdom and love and Evelyn for bringing such happiness and inspiration.

×××Tord

Martina Margetts

Thanks the following for their contributions and support:

Tord Boontje, above all

Ian Luna and Charles Miers at Rizzoli
Paul Neale at Graphic Thought Facility
Laure-Anne Maisse at Studio Boontje

The interviewees: Andrew Allenson, Paola Antonelli, Ron Arad, Juliana Barrett, Tord Boontje, Anders Byriel, Emily Campbell, Clare Catterall, Louise-Anne Comeau, Andrée Cooke, Tom Dixon, Anthony Dunne, Carina Edlund, Erwin Flototto, Hilary French, Laure Grezard, Michael Marriott, Tatjana Marsden, Julie Mathias, Simon Moore, Ulf Moritz, Patrizia Moroso, Murray Moss, Paul Neale, Joseph Nunn, Ben Panayi, Alice Rawsthorn, Simon Reynaud, Ab Rogers, Nadja Swarovski, Louise Taylor, Trino Verkade, Joke Visser van der Heyden, Daniel Weil and Emma Woffenden.

At the Royal College of Art: Professor Sir Christopher Frayling, Professor Sandra Kemp, Professor Jeremy Aynsley and Joe Kerr for supporting time to research this book; also many colleagues including Patrick Keiller, Lisa Godson, Jonathan Miles, Juliet Ash and library staff including Darlene Maxwell and Cathy Johns.

At home: Henry, Theo and Amelia Peterson, with love.

Angela

Annabel

Paul

Martina

Index

Plate photography

Annabel Elston (p. 25–29, 89–107, 109–111, 120, 138–165, 218–231 and 239–248); Angela Moore (p.1–16, 33–72, 116–119, 137, 170–184 and 201–217); Tim Tom (p. 232–237).

Other photography

All photographs by Studio Tord Boontje except: Graphic Thought Facility (cover); Luke Kirwan/ *The Guardian* (p. 82, Tord and Evie); Marcus Leith (p. 83, *Century City* installation at Tate Modern); Peter Grant (p. 84, wedding day); Creative by: Peterson Milla Hooks, Director: Steven Murashige, Animation by: Radium, Commissioned by Target (p. 87 TV advertising still); Steven Klein, art direction by Alexander McQueen (p. 125, Alexander McQueen Eyewear); Francis Ware (p. 127, Wednesday Light box); Edie Kahuila Pereira (p.131, Enrico and Tahmineh portrait); Harry Borden (p. 131, Nadja Swarovki portrait); Alessandro Paderni / Eye (p. 131, Patrizia Moroso portrait); The National Gallery, London (p. 187, Roger van der Weyden); Martin Polak (p. 250, *Wednesday*—Prague, commissioned by Andreé Cooke); V&A Photo Studio (p. 252, *Silent Light*): Alessandro Paderni/Eye (p. 256, *Happy Ever After*); Davies + Starr (p. 258–259, *The End*); Ed Reeves (p. 264, *Carousel*); Angela Moore (p. 265, *The Forest of KARAKUSA*).

First published in the United States of America by Rizzoli International Publications, Inc. 300 Park Avenue South, New York, NY 10010 www.rizzoliusa.com

Editor: Ian Luna
Production: Maria Pia Gramaglia & Kaija Markoe
Editorial Assistants: Joshua D. Jones & Chris Monroe
Designed by Graphic Thought Facility
Typeset in Vendôme and Helvetica Neue
Printed in China

2006 2007 2008 2009 / 10 9 8 7 6 5 4 3 2 1

Library of Congress Control Number: 2006940395
ISBN-10: 0–8478–2929–4
ISBN-13: 978–0–8478–2929–3